Copyright © 2017 Carol Williams

All rights reserved. This book or any
be reproduced or used in any manner
express written permission of the publisher except for the use
of brief quotations in a book review.

First Printing, 2017

ISBN-10: 1979408584
ISBN-13: 978-1979407588

Imprint: Independently published

All proceeds from the book sales (eBook or paperback) will go to the UK charity The Lily Foundation which raises funds for research into a cure for Mitochondrial Disease, and supporting families affected by Mito.
https://www.thelilyfoundation.org.uk/

Contents

Introduction	i
The Beginning	1
Trouble In Paradise	12
Harlow Wood - At Last	14
The Admission	16
The Homecoming	22
Harlow Wood - The Return	24
Our Strawberry Surprise	27
How It Used To Be — As I Remember It	30
We Are Survivors	32
As For Recycling	34
Independence	37
Our First Home	54
New Technology	82
Memories Of Children's TV.	84
Country Living	88
The Jury	96
Torquay	117
Norfolk	125
Full Circle	134
Wishes Do Come True	140
Goodbye Peter	149
Oak Court (The Hotel)	159
Mito's — How Do We Do…?	165
Some Of My Favourite Songs	169
Man's Best Friend	172
Walking Sticks	175
What is Mitochondrial disease?	177

Introduction

I thought about writing this journal many years ago, because one night after coming home from a church meeting, I was so angry at the way certain people talked down to me, I needed to vent. Just because I am physically disabled does not mean I don't have a functioning brain. I do tend to get upset with the attitude of so-called 'Normals' so I decided to write down some of what my life has been about (some dates and timings are approximations but near enough). It won't change people's attitude to disabilities but it will make me feel better. A few people may even find it interesting.

The title I chose is just as it says. It is an abbreviated story about my Life, Loves, and Living with Mitochondrial Myopathy (Mito).

To be honest when I started to write this, I have to admit to never really considering myself as disabled, just a little less strong than others. When I encountered an obstacle I usually found a way around it, so when people say, "How do you manage?" it's kind of hard to describe. I have always just accepted that there are certain things I cannot do and if I come upon something that is totally beyond me then I just asked for help.

Of course, now I am in a wheelchair full time it's a different matter, as I have gotten much worse over the years and I now HAVE to think of every move I make before making it. My life has never been easy but I have always had help and support from friends and family, so in some ways I may have been more lucky than a 'normal healthy person' and I can honestly say, despite all the difficulties I have had to encounter and overcome I really feel **Truly Blessed**, and would like to say a BIG **THANK YOU** to ALL, you know who you are.

Doctors are taught, "When you hear hoof beats, think horses, not zebras," (meaning the simplest answer is the best answer). We, the medically complicated, ARE those zebras, and we are determined to pave the way so that the next generation will have a better and easier chance at getting the proper diagnosis and care. This term was coined in the medical community before many of us were even born. All that it means is a medical 'fascinoma' which none of us readily know the definition of. For anyone who has been offended by this word, I ask that you understand that if you walk into a doctor's office and say that you are a 'zebra', you will likely get the attention of the doctor rather than if you said I have Mito. Doctors understand this term to bring their attention to the rare and fascinating conditions they do not normally see. There is no other derogatory meaning to this term and for those versed in medical language, it is to their advantage to 'know' exactly what it means.

Another little-known fact is: more children DIE from Mitochondrial Disease than they do from cancer. Why is that not talked about more? Maybe cancer is easier to say!

The Beginning

When I was born I weighed in at a whopping 10 pounds, 11 ounces. I looked normal except my hands were tightly clenched. You can just see one in the picture below.

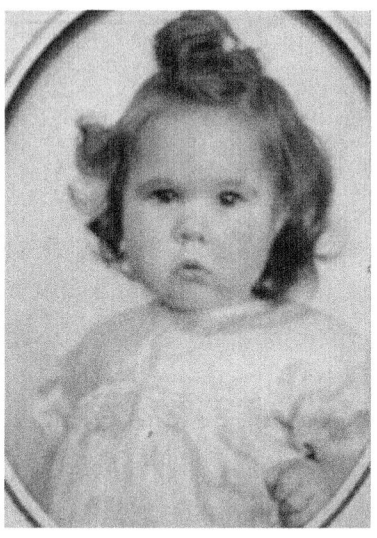

Mum said I looked like I was ready for a fight. Maybe I was born with some insight as to what sort of life I was going to have because I sure have had to do plenty of fighting since.

Apparently, no one took much notice of my hands as I was a sickly baby and indeed, when I was six months old I was critically ill in hospital with serious breathing problems. The minister from our local church was even called in to read the last rites over me. BUT HEY I am a fighter and I fought hard. I did eventually recover and was allowed home. Then my parents noticed my hands were still in tight fists and the round of visits to doctors started.

It seems no one could say why my hands were like that. My fingers would just not open unless pulled by someone else. The doctors did also notice that I was not sitting up without pillows, so over the next few months more tests were taken and the conclusion was that I had some kind of muscular disease. Therefore, I would never be strong and in fact it was doubtful I would reach the age of twenty and sorry parents but that was pushing it to the limit.

    I was the second oldest child of five to be born in our family and the only girl. None of my brothers were born with any defects or illnesses, so I guess I was the LUCKY ONE. I was four years old before I even attempted to walk; I used to shuffle around on my bottom. I went up the stairs on my hands and knees but coming down, if I didn't get on my bottom and bounce down, I usually wobbled and fell down them. For some strange reason, I always fell backwards so I kind of slid down. My balance was very tenuous, I fell over easily, one puff of wind, and I would be over, but my brothers were great, they looked after me. Of course, I still had a rough and tumble with them when we were playing. They didn't treat me like glass but did make allowances when I couldn't do something as quick as them, and when playing games like Tag, I am sure they just didn't move much at all so I could catch them. When one of them really annoyed me, I am afraid I would lose it, pick up the nearest thing to hand, and throw it at them. Mum lost quite a few ornaments that way, and if the boys were near enough, I could give a hefty punch with my closed hands. YAY! Outside, children were the opposite, and it is true, you know that saying, "Children can be very cruel." Oh boy they can!

    When I reached the grand old age of five, I had to go to school and it was one of the worst times of my life. I was teased, laughed at, name-called, bullied and just generally picked on because they knew I could not run, hop, skip, jump and play normal games. I have to say I used my illness and stayed away from school as much as possible.

Now, I have never walked properly either. To move forward I had to sort of swing my legs and really concentrate. One day walking home, I wasn't concentrating enough and I fell, breaking my arm in the process. The pain was horrendous. One of the neighbours saw me fall and called the ambulance which came and took me to hospital where they put on a plaster cast so I was fixed up enough to go home but joy of joys I was told I didn't have to go back to school until my arm was better. Oh yes, it hurt, but worth it for that one reason, a reprieve that lasted for six whole weeks.

While my arm was in plaster, doctors commented on my fingers being bent and wanted to do some tests. They did and could find nothing wrong and said I would probably grow out of it. What a laugh — but, we are talking about the early 1950s.

There must have been a social welfare officer at the hospital who the doctor talked to, because my parents had a visit from them, asking if it would be better if I went to the special school down the road. The pupils there were all disabled, most were in wheelchairs. But to outsiders my dad was in total denial and said, "There is nothing wrong with my daughter and if she went to that school she would end up like them. No, she will go to the normal school as before." Shame nobody asked me. I would love to have gone where I would have been accepted. Of course, Mum never got to say anything because Dad was the boss. We all had to do what he said, and yet indoors he did treat me like glass and would not let me do anything he thought might hurt me. He would not even let me have any of the inoculations that the boys had. He said, "Nobody is putting anything into my daughter that might endanger her life." Talk about confused, I certainly was.

So, when my arm was fully recovered I had to go back to the taunting. The teachers were great and very helpful but sometimes that made it worse because then I was called "teacher's pet." Sometimes I really hated my dad for putting me through all that. Although on reflection, I think maybe I should have thanked him, because I am sure it made me a much stronger person than I might have been.

Every winter was guaranteed to see me with chilblains, styes on my eyes (very uncomfortable and sore). I would come down with bronchitis that nearly always turned into pneumonia. The nurse used to come around three times every day and stick a big needle in my thigh (and I mean BIG, not like the fine little syringes we have today). Boy was it painful. Then I had to go onto something they called an A-frame, which I had to bend over forwards while my parents took it in turns tapping and rubbing my back to encourage me to bring up stuff that was lodged in my lungs. It was horrendous and I think they hated it nearly as much as I did.

Of course, the air pollution was much worse in those days, during winter months, as we all had coal fires bellowing out thick smoke. The fogs were so thick, sometimes seeing a hand in front of you was difficult — funnily enough I used to love foggy days, it was like being in a secret world. I felt so elated because no one could see how awkwardly I walked, so I relished those times and went out as much as I was allowed with my scarf over my nose and mouth (just like a bandit)! At least we didn't have the car pollution, as there were not many around; cars were a luxury for the well-to-do, which we certainly were not.

In fact, I remember Dad going out hunting for rabbit and pigeon with his friend Harry. When he came home with their catch we all had to help skin the rabbits, pluck the pigeons and gut the lot. It was a very smelly, messy process, but Dad said we had to learn these things for our own good. We also had some hens wandering around in the yard and garden and we had to go and find the eggs. Dad used to clip the hens' wings so they couldn't fly out of the garden and when they had reached the time they no longer laid eggs we prepared them for the cook pot. Mum was very good at making delicious meals from these, added to the vegetables Dad grew all year. We also had to go out and pick berries — blackberries, blackcurrant, elder and dandelion flowers — for Dad to make his own wine and hops for his beer. It seemed that things grew in abundance back then, so for some of the year we felt very rich indeed.

The winters REALLY were fierce. The snow could be up to four feet deep and the frost was always on the INSIDE of the windows during the nights.

We children all used to sleep in the same room which was a bit cosier. My oldest brother had a single bed and we three younger ones in a double bed. I always slept in the middle and during those long cold winters I was VERY glad to, it was the warmest place to be. Sometimes when we were not sleepy we would play a game we called 'picture back'. We used to lay on our sides and finger draw a picture on the back in front of you. The person would then have to guess what was being drawn.

Then we would turn over and do it all again. Of course, being in the middle meant that I had to draw more but I got to be drawn on more too. It was a very relaxing, quiet thing to do. However, as we grew our parents got some new beds so we could all have one each. They were two sets of bunk beds and we used to have some fun laying there making up stories after lights out. One night near Christmas, one of my brothers said, "Look, there's Santa and the reindeers flying over the fields," (we all used to lay facing the window) and when we looked it really did look like Santa and the reindeer. It was obviously a cloud formation but we believed in Santa then.

Of course, we had to be wary of the "Bogeyman" — if we were not asleep by a certain time, he was sure to come and get us. One night our dad came into the room and told us we had been making too much noise and it was past time to be asleep. He told us goodnight again and we thought he had gone because it all went quiet. We started giggling and telling stories when, all of a sudden in the darkness, a booming voice said, "You were told to go to sleep!" Well, we all lay there in the total darkness terrified and went totally silent, not even daring to move in case it was the Bogeyman! Then our Dad said, "Now shut up and sleep!" Then he really did leave the room knowing we were now too scared to make a sound. It's no wonder that when eventually I had to sleep in my own room that I had nightmares. I used to think there was a crocodile under my bed waiting for me to move so he could come out and eat me up and I really did believe I felt him pushing my mattress up to get me out. I sure did scream when that happened.

Then there was the time my parents bought me a huge doll. She was nearly as big as me and I was supposed to use her as my model for making clothes, which I had a desire to do. My gran had given me her old sewing machine and lots of pieces of material so I was good to go. This huge doll used to stand in the corner of my room and at nights I could see her from my bed as the street light was right outside my window and when I looked at her I could swear I saw her blink and as I was dozing off I thought I heard her move. Once again, my imagination went into overdrive and I honestly thought this doll was coming to get me. I lay there screaming in terror. Just moving the doll out of the room was no good. She had to go!

My mother gave birth to another son and while she had been carrying him, I asked her if we could have a baby girl so I could have a sister because if it was another boy — I was leaving home, she said, "Let's wait and see, shall we?" Well, when the time came and he arrived she asked me if I was going to pack a bag because it was another boy, then she held him out to me and asked if I wanted to hold him before I left, which I did with

Mum's help. I took one look at his beautiful face and said, "I think I will stay."

When my youngest brother was old enough to go into his own bed, he didn't like it, so I was given the job of going to bed with him and tell him stories. I told him he was in a special bed, it used to be mine and there was nothing to worry about.

When he fell asleep, I could get up and go back downstairs until it was my bedtime, which meant I had to go into my own room now. The boys all slept in one room as I had done before. Now I was coming up to the grand age of ten and apparently, I needed my own room — to be honest I felt like I had been punished and banned and I did so miss my siblings' company. Mum said it was for my own good now I was growing up and was too old to share the boys' room. So, the decision was made and there was no arguing with parents. I had to settle down to a life of solitude and of course eventually I did adjust and after a while I did enjoy my own space.

I had moved up to the senior school now and this was an all girls' school. I noticed the girls didn't torment me so much without the boys around; in fact, I even made a few friends, all of them wanting to look after and protect me.

This school was much bigger than the juniors'. There were three storeys and we had to move around the building to go to different lessons. As it took me longer to get to the next lesson, I always had to leave one classroom a few minutes earlier, so I was already up the stairs before the bell went and everyone came charging up or down to get to their next class. I still hated school and took as much time off as I could, usually by telling my parents I wasn't feeling well. The 'board man' would come around to the house if I had been off for too long, to see why I wasn't at school. Usually Mum was home and could tell him. I asked her what the board man was and she explained he was in charge of seeing who was really ill at home or if they were playing truant and getting into trouble.

Oh, and now we had a motor car. Dad had found someone who would lend him the money to buy one. He bought a Morris Minor Traveller and every Saturday afternoon the money lender came for a cup of tea and his payment. I didn't like him one bit, he sat there smoking his pipe as if he owned the place. Nearly every adult we knew smoked. Our house was always smoky — it was considered sociable (I am sure the non-smoking lobbyists of today would have a lot to say about it).

Having a car gave us some freedom. Instead of walking over 'The Western Park' to visit my grandma and all my aunties, we all piled in the car and got there much quicker which meant we had more time to spend with them. I used to love my grandad, he was a very quiet man, he never stayed indoors long as he tended his garden most of the day. I thought it was because he loved gardening but my dad said not, it was to escape Grandma. I didn't understand then what he meant, but one day he had a BIG argument with his mum and took us all home. The last thing he ever said to her was, "You will need me before I need you. You may talk to your husband like dirt but you're not doing that to me!" And that was the last time I saw them for many years as Dad banned us from going over. It was a few years before I found out what went wrong and it was just about getting her the wrong type of brandy.

On a brighter note, now instead of going on the train for our holiday to Snettisham, we went further afield to Crantock in Cornwall. First, we went camping, then after a couple of years we changed to a caravan. The drive down used to take 12 hours as there were no motorways. Our luggage was sent on by the train to await pickup at the station when we all got down there. We had the Morris Minor Traveller and Dad used to put a mattress in the back, we kids would pile in and go to sleep while he drove us. Dad used to hold the steering wheel so tight he had blisters on his hands when we got there — makes you wonder if it was all worth it. But we had to have our two weeks at the seaside it seems, and to be honest Cornwall is a great place to go.

The beaches were beautiful and clean. Mum and Dad would pack a picnic basket full of food and we spent many days on the beach. There were lots of caves to explore.

Some were enormous. When you looked up they seemed to go on forever and there was writing and pictures on the walls. None of us understood any of it but it was fascinating. The boys wanted to go right in and explore as far as they could to see if they could find some hidden treasure but I was too scared to leave the sight of the beach; I had read where the tide comes in so fast you could get trapped and drown. Well, that's not what I wanted so I stayed near the entrances. The many rock pools were full of interesting plants, fish and crabs, I preferred those to the caves.

The Atlantic Ocean would come crashing in and for those who could swim they went through the waves with delight then come out hungry again so we would pack up and meander through the sand dunes back to the tent or caravan where Mum would cook a fabulous dinner. Sometimes Dad took the boys out in a fishing boat for the day and again Mum cooked their catch when they brought it home.

I used to read quite a bit too, one of my favourite books was written by Hans Christian Andersen. One of the stories I really liked was 'The Little Mermaid'. It was about a mermaid who wished she could walk like humans as she thought having legs would be the best thing ever. As I read this story I used to wish I could swap places and have her fabulous tail and swim around all the time (most little girls dream of being a ballerina — me, I wanted to be a mermaid).

One year when we were on our annual holiday they held a Fancy Dress competition in the village. My parents decided to make my wish come true for a short while. They wrapped my legs up in crepe paper and made a fish tail to put my feet in. As I had very long hair I was allowed to have it down and flowing on my back and chest with no clothes on the top (good job it was a warm sunny day) then they put me on one of those trolleys you see in garden centres, decorated it with plants and fishes and when it was time to parade Dad pulled me along for all to see. I never won the competition but it was all such good fun. It also made me realise how lucky I was to have legs, even if they didn't work very well at least I could still use them.

I still got ill every autumn and when I was eleven years old, our doctor told my parents the reason he thought I was so ill was because I had such long hair (to date I had never had it cut and I was able to sit on it). He said it was making me weak by taking all my strength away, so he recommended I have it cut. My dad was devastated. I was elated, as I was always getting it pulled at school by the bullies and the knots were painful when Mum was brushing it. So, for me it was great. Dad took me to the hairdresser and I had it cut short into my neck. It did feel really strange but also, I felt light-headed and free.

Here I am in Bridlington with my Dad and brother Michael, it was so nice to feel the wind blowing my short hair around.

Trouble In Paradise

Also, when I was eleven, something really bad happened in my life and it had nothing to do with my health. It was to do with my oldest brother, who was thirteen and some would say an early developer. He started to visit me in my room when everyone was asleep. At first, he said it was to talk because he couldn't sleep, and then he would get under the covers and started touching me in places I knew he shouldn't. When I asked, "What are you doing?" His reply was, "Oh come on! I need some practice on how to make out with girls and you're perfect for it."

I couldn't believe I was hearing right and told him so; also, it just wasn't right what he wanted between brother and sister. His reply was, "It doesn't matter" because he was only my half-brother, apparently, he had found his birth certificate in Mum's bureau and the name of his father was not the same as ours. His father was an American Air Force pilot. This was another shock, I had no idea (and indeed why would I)? But that would explain why Dad always called him "That little bastard." I told my brother that still did not make it right for him to get into my bed, but he would not leave me alone and as he was bigger and a lot stronger than me he had his wicked way whenever he felt like it.

So, I lost my virginity and my peace of mind. Now I dreaded night times. It went on for months until one night I made more fuss than usual and Mum heard. She came to my room, saw us and told my brother to get back to his own bed and never let her catch us doing that again. She told me never to mention this to another soul and just went back to her room. I felt terribly embarrassed but so glad Chris had been found out and I thought now Mum knows that will be the end of his visits.

I was hoping that really was the case but my brother had other ideas. After a few weeks, he started his visits again. He told me to be quiet or else I would know real trouble. I was terrified of him and of being caught again, so I did everything he wanted but every night I cried and wondered when this was going to stop. I felt my life was hell and wished I could get away.

This is what they call sexual abuse, incest or rape today, and there is help, but then I had no one to turn to, not even my mum. She said she didn't want to talk about it. Had my dad known he would have killed my brother I'm sure, moreover, as it was all such a very painful and shameful experience I have not gone into any details as to the things he did to me, though I will never forget them for as long as I live. Tony is the only person I ever told and that was before we got married, as I did not want him thinking he had married a virgin on our wedding night, and when years later my brother died of cancer, strangely I did not cry at his funeral.

Harlow Wood - At Last

My wish finally came true, and the escape from my brother came from a double blessing. My brother was accepted into the Royal Navy. He signed up for nine years, at last able to follow his dream. Maybe now he would be happy. And also from a doctor who was interested in my hands and wanted to do something to try and put them right, so I could use them. His name was Mr Reginald Pulvertaft.

The very first time I saw him I was frightened. He was sitting on a stool at a tiny table in the middle of a huge, almost bare room. Behind him were a group of people (later I found out they were doctors, anaesthetists, physiotherapists, etc.) He said, "Hello Carol, come on over and sit here in front of me." That walk across the room seemed so long. Well, I got onto the other stool and looked into his eyes. They seemed very far away because he was wearing thick glasses, but he had a nice, soothing voice and as soon as he took hold of my hands I felt safe. He said, "Put your hands on the table so we can take a good look at them." When he said that all these other people came forward and stood looking at us. He introduced them as his team who will all be helping me get my fingers working. After giving my hands a good examination, he asked if I would wait outside with my parents while he discussed with his team what he wanted to do to help. Eventually he called us back in and said he could help but it would mean quite a few operations. All would be painful and none of this was guaranteed to work. Also, I had a choice to make: He could give me perfect straight fingers but they would not work anymore than my clenched ones did now or he could make my fingers work, but they would not be perfectly straight, so I had to choose — did I want to go through all the pain for straight or working fingers? I chose to go for the working model and knew I would tolerate the pain for something so important. So, it was decided.

Mr Pulvertaft was based in Derby but because of my weak chest he wanted me to go to an open-air hospital. The nearest one was Mansfield, called Harlow Wood Orthopaedic Hospital. It seemed to be a very long way from home (but was in fact only about 46 miles). It took over two hours to arrive by car. Of course, there were no motorways in those days and cars didn't go very fast, not like they do now, which is probably why it took so long. I had to go there for another interview with Mr Pulvertaft so he could explain exactly what they were going to do to help me.

When we turned into the drive sweeping uphill from the main road, the sight was amazing: both sides of the drive were full of trees and shrubs, with blazing, beautiful-coloured flowers of pinks, blues, yellow, peach, red, and purple, it looked magical. Dad told me they were rhododendrons — camellias, azalea and hydrangeas, the colours were fabulous. At the top of the drive was the nurses' home, then it curved to the right towards a car park and the main building where the reception, clinic rooms, operating theatre, offices and kitchens were. Opposite that building was a workshop where they made the splints, leg irons, etc. Next to that was the swimming pool. The whole hospital was completely surrounded by a thick forest of trees. When the clinic was finished Dad was told we would get a letter telling us when to go back for my admission to Mansfield for the start of my operations.

The Admission

So, here I am in a very different sort of hospital from any I have ever been in before. It has the big main building as normal with lots of rooms including the operating theatre, lots of offices and such but the wards are all separate units and are connected with covered pathways.

Dad says again that we are in the middle of Sherwood Forest where Robin Hood used to live and as I look around, I see hundreds of trees. I am taken past the first building, which is Ward 1 (for babies and toddlers), and into Ward 2 (for 7 to 15 years). To me it seems massive and the whole of one side is wide open to a sunny veranda. Good job it is a sunny day, the fresh air coming in is good, it is late September and I had my thirteenth birthday in July. I am taken to a bed and told this is where I will be staying for the next few weeks, so my dad unpacks my bag and talks to me for a little bit then he says he has got to go home to Mum and the boys. Now I am not too sure I want to stay here on my own, but the kind nurse who came in with us, told me I would not be alone with all these other children around and Dad has to go.

So I started a new adventure and here the children were not nasty or tormenting. I wondered if that is because we all have something wrong with us. The nurse was right, I am not alone and there is plenty for us to play with but I was wondering about the wall being open and was told the doors are open for much of the day to give us lots of fresh air, which is one way of clearing poorly chests in people who get bronchitis (which I was one of). I was having so much fun until that Monday when a strange lady came up to me and said, "I am the teacher and will be giving you your lessons." (Oh no! I didn't know they had schools in hospital, I thought I had escaped them.) Well, I just looked at her and said, "I cannot do any writing because I am having my hand operated on in the morning." She took one look at me and said, "Well my dear, that's no problem, you have another hand, you can learn to use that!" Which is exactly what I did do. So now I have another skill, I am ambidextrous.

As children do, we got into mischief sometimes. I remember one night when Matron was doing her rounds, a few of us had 'borrowed' some syringes, (they didn't have the needles on) without permission of course and we filled them with water and ejected it into the air. Some of it hit Matron as she was walking around. She was not amused and the punishment she gave us was — she stopped us from watching television for a whole week, and of course television was still very new in those days so that was a big punishment for us.

The Sister on our ward was wonderful, her name was Sister Walgrave, she too lived in Leicester and on her off-duty weekends she went home. Sometimes she took me with her and dropped me off at home, so I could spend some time with my family and then she would come and take me back to the hospital.

The first operation was on my right hand because it was the worst affected. I had to have the skin on my fingers stretched by cutting in a 'Z' shape on the inside of each finger. Mr Pulvertaft had to be careful not to stretch them too far so as to cause nerve damage. Both my hands were bad but like I said the right was the worst and that was the one they started on and if it didn't work then I had lost nothing but, if all the procedures worked (and there were many) on that hand then they would start on the left eventually.

As we lived so far away, I only had visitors one day a week, which was usually a Sunday. Dad brought the whole family sometimes and others it was just him and Mum. I got used to only seeing them for a short period as there was so much to do and everyone was so nice, I didn't seem to miss them all as much as I thought I would. I really did enjoy my stay, even though the operations were painful and the physiotherapy was very hard. I had to go four times a day for physio to keep my fingers supple, ready for the next phase.

Christmas came and the atmosphere was incredible. We made lots and lots of decorations for the ward during school time. All the staff put on a pantomime for us, there was so much joy and laughter you would have found it hard to believe we were all in a hospital. We had a full Christmas dinner and many presents from the Salvation Army and other benefactors. We all sang carols. Oh, it was just wonderful! Everyone who had relatives came for a while too. I don't think I have ever enjoyed a party as much as that one.

After all the festivities were over and things got back to normal, it was time for the next phase of my treatment which was to have tendons taken from my left foot and put into my right hand, joining them at the wrist and knuckles. This was a very long and complicated procedure; the operation took 8 hours. They also took a muscle biopsy from my right leg to see what was wrong with my muscles. When the results came back I heard Muscular Dystrophy but didn't understand what they meant.

When I woke from the operation I had a plaster splint on, but there were little slings attached to elastic hanging from a wire frame. I soon found out I had to pull on these to keep my fingers from setting and to stop the tendons from shrinking, also to strengthen them. This was a very painful procedure and I had to persevere. The physio took months because I had to learn how to use my fingers, which was something I had never been able to do, so it was all new to me too.

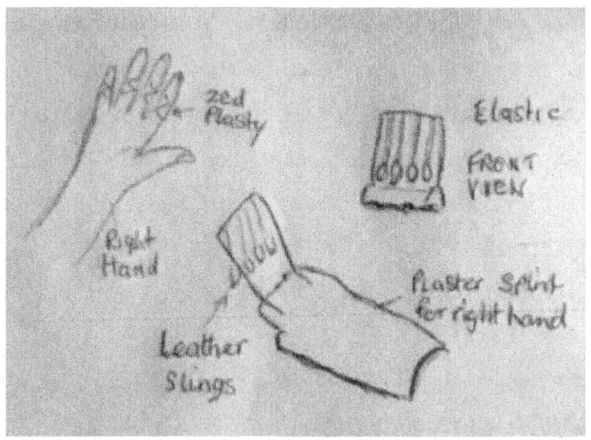

There were also two manipulations that had to be done, because my fingers did set and would not move. Also during this time, we had to move out of Ward 2 (the reason we had to move was they knocked down Ward 2 and built a brand new operating theatre, which at the time was state-of-the-art, much bigger and brighter than the old one).

We older children were transferred to Ward 4, which was mainly for private patients, so were told we had to be quiet a lot of the time and not disturb the private patients.

I had my fourteenth birthday there, along with three others and it was such fun. All our parents bought us a string puppet, so we could make our own shows (I wanted Gretel from Hansel and Gretel but they had sold out and I ended up with Pinocchio. I still have him today in his original box).

Now one of the other girls named Pauline was mad keen on the singer Joe Brown and she wrote to the fan club and asked if Joe would come to the hospital to play for us on our birthday, (thinking he never would) but surprise, surprise, he did. He came on his own with his guitar, as the Bruvvers were playing elsewhere. Sister and the nurses had lots of food prepared so we had a fabulous party with Joe singing and playing our requests. All staff who weren't too busy came to watch and considering we had to be very quiet on this ward, that one day we all made lots of noise and even the private patients came and joined in.

Joe Brown was a very friendly, happy person, and his coming to visit was another great day in our painful lives. He made us all feel so special and loved and little Pauline who was the happiest fan EVER. She had a silly smile on her face for weeks. and went around saying (in her Geordie accent) "Awe Joe I love you so."

Mr Pulvertaft was very pleased with how my operations had taken and as I had worked hard with the physiotherapists and occupational therapy too, I showed him all the things I had made in the OT department using my newly operational fingers (yes, now my fingers worked — although they were not as straight as normal, at least I could now pick up things and feed myself, I had also learnt to embroider, sew, paint and draw, and this was only one hand done). He said I could go home for a few weeks, to give me and my parents a break and while I was gone he and his team would get everything ready for starting the left hand. So, in March off I went back home for a while.

Explanation for overseas readers: During the 1960s, children's schooling was in four stages, Nursery age 3-5, Infants age 5-7, Junior age 7-11 and Senior age 11-14 depending on where your birthday fell during the year you either started school in Spring or Autumn. The only people that went on to further education and university were the really clever ones or the rich. The rest got jobs and worked a 40-hour week minimum. There were plenty of jobs in those days. Now it is different, they have to stay in school until they are 18 and there are not many jobs.

The Homecoming

It was too late for me to go back to school as I was only supposed to be home for a few weeks. Well, a few weeks turned into a few months, and to help pass the time while I was waiting to go back to Harlow Wood, I went to our local infant school and talked with the headmistress, Mrs Griffiths. She was a lovely, caring lady and so popular with all people not only because she loved all the children in her care and knew all their names but also because she always had her little Scottish Terrier following close behind at her heel. Wherever she went so did her little dog. His name was Shadow (I wonder why). One of her pupils who had now grown up to be a young man had actually painted Shadow in oils and presented it to Mrs Griffiths who proudly hung it up in the main hall of the school for all to see.

It was good to talk with Mrs Griffiths, and tell her my boredom problem. She was a good listener. She came up with a wonderful solution to my boredom that would also help her and that was for me to help in the nursery class. Of course, I would get no pay, as I was untrained. I said that was no problem if I could work there without pay, I just needed something to help pass the time away while waiting to go back into hospital. She said she had to get head office approval, if they allowed it then she would be delighted for me to help look after the pre-school (nursery) children. They did allow it as long as I realised I could not be paid. So it was settled, I was officially a helper in class. Now that was really fun. One of the biggest surprises for me when I first started at the school was how the children manipulated their parents. They could cry their eyes out and the tears would flow, making the parents feel very guilty about leaving their poor little babies, but in actual fact as soon as the parents had turned their backs the children forgot all about them and enjoyed playing with the other children. (It was a lesson I remembered well when I took my own children to their first school.)

I also never realised how much work pre-school (nursery) teachers did and how much they actually do for the small children, from teaching them how to draw, read and write, we also had to teach them how to use a knife, fork and spoon as they all stayed for a cooked meal at lunch time. After the meal and a little play, all the children had their own camp bed which they laid down in for a rest. Most went to sleep for an hour and while the children rested we adults sat sewing motifs on their aprons and tunics and repaired damaged ones, we also prepared things for the next day's activities. It was great fun but also very tiring and when 4.00pm came round, evening prayers had been said and all the children had gone off with their parents, we too headed home.

Of course, my dad was not happy that I was doing this every day and not getting paid for it. I told him I was getting paid, not in money it's true, but experience and something to do now I was too old for school myself and no-one would hire me for work because I would have had to leave when Mr Pulvertaft called me back to Harlow Wood, which could be any time. It was a lovely experience and when it really was time for me to go back into hospital, Mrs Griffiths the headmistress told me I had a natural aptitude for helping the children and if, when I was finally finished with the hospital, I wanted to train as a professional nursery teacher, then she would recommend me to the best teacher training school which was in London. Well, I thought that was very nice of her, and I said I would let her know when I finally came home. I thanked her for letting me help in the nursery. It had been an invaluable experience for me.

Harlow Wood - The Return

So here I am once again in Harlow Wood. When we arrived at reception, I was told to go to Ward 7.

Sister Bebe was in charge. She was a short person with a round, happy face and dark hair. She had a lovely Welsh accent and told Mum and Dad that I would be spoilt rotten as I was the youngest patient on the ward (as I am now sixteen years old and am looked upon as grown up and not a child any more). The older ladies did spoil me but I too tried to help them whenever I could because I was an 'up-patient' which meant that I wasn't confined to bed all day. So my days of playing are over but having fun was still on the cards, after all we were in the middle of a forest, the sun was shining and there were a few other older teenage girls on the ward and luckily for us we all got on really well.

Two of the girls (Wendy and Sue) were like me and able to walk about but the other (Pam) was stuck in bed a lot. She was born with one leg four inches shorter than the other, so she was in to have her longer leg shortened and her shorter leg stretched to try and make them near the same size. We did our OT together, usually sitting around Pam's bed when she couldn't get out. When she could, we would get a wheelchair and push her around the hospital grounds. In this photo, the Orderly was named June; she pushed Pam outside the ward and I am holding the ward's mascot.

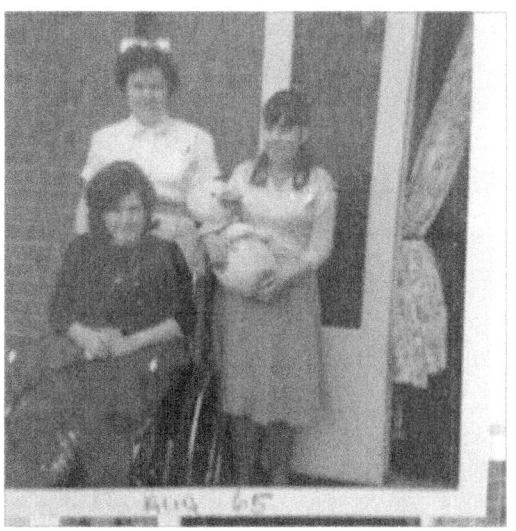

Now, Ward 7 was right at the edge of the hospital near the main road into Mansfield and we had to pass all the other wards to get to the swimming pool which just happened to be right next to the men's wards. Sometimes when we were feeling really daring, we would bypass the swimming pool and go to the men's ward and start chatting with them. As most of us were far away from home we all appreciated a visit and a good chat, mostly the staff didn't mind either as they said it helped boost morale.

There were some nice young men in there, sometimes a couple of them would come out with us and we would all go for a lovely long walk through the forest. There were many paths, not all were twisty, some were really straight and seemed to go on for miles, they were easy to push Pam through in the wheelchair. The days passed so quickly and before we knew it, it was winter. The snow came thick and fast. In those days and we didn't go out into the woods so much, though it was still so idyllic listening to the birds singing and sometimes we would see a badger or a fox pass us by.

Our Strawberry Surprise

It was on a sunny day in February when we were all sitting out on the veranda, Sister Bebe had said we should get out and enjoy the fresh air. Wards 5 through to 10 were not the same as 1-4, the walls didn't open up they had French doors instead. Nurses pushed the beds out and we who could walk took our chairs out. Now our veranda is overlooking the main road into Mansfield. There is quite a slope to get up to us and the snow was laying deeply all around us and we were all having a laugh at something someone had said when suddenly a car stopped and a man got out and took something from the back of his car, then he started to climb up to us. Well, we called for Sister Bebe to come over and she got to us just as the man got onto the veranda (now Sister Bebe is only a small lady but no one messes with her). She went up to this man and said, "What are you doing on hospital grounds?" (She's Welsh and I think the dragon was rearing up). The poor man looked terrified but he stood his ground and said, "I am sorry to intrude but as I was driving by I saw all these ladies looking so happy I wanted to share their joy and I thought you might like these for your tea," with which he then presented sister with a REALLY BIG basket full of fresh strawberries.

    WOW. Strawberries in winter — what a treat. Apparently, he was a salesman for a food company and was on his way to a shop to try and sell them and feeling very sorry for himself having to work with all the snow around but seeing us all so happy, made him feel very humble. Sister accepted his gift and sent one of the nurses off to the shop to get some fresh cream. The man (never did know his name) stayed and shared our tea and we all made him laugh. He even helped wheel the beds back into the ward. When it was time for him to go, he said he "...would never forget this happy scene of all you beautiful ladies sitting out and looking so happy, even though we were in hospital". Now that truly was an experience we all enjoyed and such a happy memory to keep forever.

Much the same happened with my left hand as had my right, only this time they had more idea what they were doing. As my right hand had been experimental, they had taken films of all the procedures as they went along. Mr Pulvertaft didn't actually do any of the operations this time, because his eyesight was failing and some of it was micro-surgery. He supervised while his assistant did the work. He did always promise me that none of my scars would show too much and he kept his word. They did such fine cuts none were too visible, but to be honest I was not too bothered if people did see them as I was quite proud of my new hands and how I could now use them. I don't think I will ever forget the look on his face when I showed him my first hand-knitted jumper (the ladies on the ward had taught me how to knit). Who was more proud, him or me? It was a wonderful moment; we all had tears in our eyes.

I was discharged from the hospital shortly after my seventeenth birthday. As I was about to leave the clinic Mr Pulvertaft told me there was going to be a doctors' convention in a few weeks' time and as one of his protégées, he asked if I would come along so he could "show me off". Of course, I said I would go, he had done so much for me.

I got the invite a few weeks later. Dad took me. We did not know what to expect and while waiting in the foyer, I saw in the next room a film being shown. I recognised it as one of my operations. I wanted to watch it. The room was full of doctors from all over the world and I was fascinated by it all. After the film ended Mr Pulvertaft called me over to a desk and asked if I would show the doctors my hands. They asked many questions and by the end of the day I was feeling exhausted.

I found out from one of the staff there had been over 400 doctors in attendance. Mr Pulvertaft came over to me before we left and thanked me for being so patient. I said, "It should be me thanking you for all you have done for me and for giving me the chance to be here today," and his reply was "For you, it was a pleasure. Now go home and start your new life." Which is exactly what I did.

Now, before I go too far forward, I would like to add a few memories of how life was in our younger days and some of you will remember them too.

How It Used To Be — As I Remember It

For people of a certain age these things will be familiar and to the younger folks some of whom would think this is all make believe... **it was not.**

Just after World War II, there were still food shortages for many years. There were many illnesses and only the strongest survived. Summers were hot and winters were very cold. Jack Frost even came on the inside of our windows, our blankets were frozen to our faces sometimes (no duvets then). There was no central heating, we only had one open fire in the lounge and we were lucky if our parents could afford some coal. Which in the winter made bad air when it was foggy. They called it smog. There were no carpets on the floor just Lino.

Food was kept fresh in the pantry on a cold slab. We had no fridges or washing machines. Chocolate and sweets were a REAL treat and very rare. If you ran out of sugar or milk, you knew a neighbour would lend you some until you got to the shops next day. We all helped each other when in need. No power tools for the DIY or Health and Safety regulations, just plain common sense. The local police could cuff you around the ear if you were caught doing wrong and if your parents heard about it you got into trouble again for getting into trouble.

Until the mid-1950s we didn't have TV or a car, as they were all luxuries. There was no traffic to worry about. Children used their imaginations when it came to play, which was outside most of the time (no lounging around for us indoors) making their own games, like hop-scotch, marbles, whip-and-top, cowboys and Indians, tag, hide-and-seek. We never worried about strangers on the street and we could leave our homes unlocked. When I was telling my twelve-year-old grandson this he looked shocked and said, "Didn't you worry about burglars coming in?" I replied, "No, because nobody had anything worth stealing." Even parks and churches were not locked. People were more friendly and trusting.

Our lives were simple and some would say hard. An obese child was a rarity but we all got on well most of the time and played happily. Of course, there were arguments and fights but nothing as nasty as happens now, we soon made up and forgot it. Our parents struggled to make ends meet but somehow they always did, even to the extent of having a holiday every year, for two whole weeks at the seaside.

It wasn't until the late 1970s/80s that things like remote control TV, microwaves, more cars, double-glazing, and central-heating came on to the scene, along with new and virulent illnesses before unknown. The 90s to now for mobile phones, personal computers, MP3s, iPods, iPads, etc., and all the other things that make life so much different these days like, isolation and being unsocial. But with all the affluence and technology of today I wonder sometimes who was better off?

We Are Survivors

We were born before television, before antibiotics, polio shots, frozen foods, Xerox, contact lenses, videos and the pill. We were before radar, credit cards, split atoms, laser beams and ballpoint pens, before dishwashers, tumble dryers, electric blankets, air-conditioners, drip-dry clothes and before man walked on the moon.

We were married first and then lived together (how quaint can you be?). We thought fast food was what you gave up in Lent. (How many even know what Lent is anymore?) A big Mac was an oversized raincoat, and "crumpet" a kind of dough cake we had for tea. We existed before house-husbands, computer dating and shelters were where you waited for a bus.

We were before day-care centres, group homes and disposable nappies. We never had FM radio, tape decks, artificial hearts, word processors or young men wearing earrings. For us time-sharing meant togetherness, the chip was a piece of walnut or fried potato, hardware meant nuts and bolts and software wasn't a word.

Before 1940, made in Japan meant junk, the term 'making out' referred to how you did in your exams, stud was something that fastened to a collar of a shirt and going all the way meant staying on a double-decker bus to the terminus. In our day cigarette smoking was fashionable, grass was mown, coke was kept in the coal house, and a joint was a piece of meat you ate on Sundays and pot was something you cooked in. Rock music was a fond mother's lullaby, Eldorado was an ice cream, a gay person was the life and soul of the party while 'aids' just meant beauty treatments or help for someone in trouble.

Those of us who were born during the 1940s must be a hardy bunch when you think of the way in which the world has changed and the adjustments we have had to make. No wonder there is a generation gap today, but by the grace of God, we have survived.

As For Recycling
I remember it well

Checking out at the grocery shop recently, the young cashier suggested I should bring my own grocery bags because plastic bags were not good for the environment. I replied, "Yes recycling is needed more these days than when we were younger."

The clerk responded, "That's our problem today. Your generation did not care enough to save our environment for future generations." She was right about one thing — our generation did not have the recycling thing as such, in 'our' day.

So, what did we have back then? After some reflection and soul-searching on 'our' day here's what I remembered we did have. Back then, we returned milk, pop and beer bottles to the shop. The shop sent them back to the depot to be washed, sterilised and refilled. They could use the same bottles repeatedly. So, they really were recycled.

We walked up stairs, because we didn't have an escalator in every store and office building. We walked to the grocery shop and didn't climb into a high-powered, fuel-thirsty vehicle every time we had to travel a few yards. Back then, we washed the baby's nappies because we didn't have the throw-away kind. We dried clothes on a line, not in an energy-gobbling machine burning up 240 volts — wind and solar power really did dry our clothes back in our early days.

Kids got hand-me-down clothes from their brothers or sisters, not always brand-new clothing.

Back then, we had one TV, or radio, in the house — not a TV in every room, and the TV had a small screen the size of a handkerchief (remember them? No tissues for us) not the huge screens we have now. In the kitchen, we blended and stirred by hand because we didn't have electric machines to do everything for us. When we packaged a fragile item to send in the mail, we used wadded up old newspapers to cushion it, not styrofoam or plastic bubble-wrap.

Back then, we didn't fire up an engine and burn petrol just to cut the lawn. We used a push mower that ran on human power. We exercised by working, so we didn't need to go to a health club, to run on treadmills that operate on electricity. We drank from a fountain when we were thirsty, instead of using a cup or a plastic bottle every time we had a drink of water. We refilled writing pens with ink instead of buying a new pen, and we replaced the razor blades in a razor instead of throwing away the whole razor just because the blade got dull.

Back then, people took the tram or a bus, and kids rode their bikes to school or walked instead of turning their parents into a 24-hour taxi service. We had one electrical outlet in a room, not an entire bank of sockets to power a dozen appliances. We didn't need a computerised gadget to receive a signal beamed from satellites 2,000 miles out in space in order to find the nearest pizza joint.

But isn't it sad that the current generation laments how wasteful we old folks were just because we didn't call it recycling or being GREEN? People are always willing to put the blame onto someone else.

It reminds me of this little story I heard in Church one day:

This is the story about four people named **Everybody, Somebody, Anybody & Nobody.** There was an important job to be done and **Everybody** was sure **Somebody** would do it. **Anybody** could have done it but **Nobody** did. Now **Somebody** got angry about that because it was **Everybody's** job. **Everybody** thought **Anybody** could do it but **Nobody** realised that **Everybody** wouldn't do it. It ended up that **Everybody** blamed **Somebody** when **Nobody** did what **Anybody** could have done.

And that's the way it is.

Independence

I had decided I had been away from home for too long already and going down to London for two years' teacher training was out. Now came the tricky bit, I wanted to go out to work but my dad said he didn't want me to join the rat-race, and I was going to stay home so he could look after me. Hmmm, I didn't like the sound of that. He did allow me to apply to art college as I had learnt I had a talent for drawing while I was in the hospital. I had a few appointments for interviews at some local colleges, but either I didn't like them or I did not have what they wanted, so we widened the search area. After all there were many art colleges in England, I have to admit some of them were very daunting and huge with their high ceilings and long sweeping staircases, I felt totally out of my depth.

A friend suggested we go and look at a special place in Reading. It was a bit further away but sounded great. When we got there the college wasn't so big and the people were very friendly. They liked my work too. Best of all, they had a group of bungalows completely adapted for disabled people to live in during their time of studying. Each bungalow was shared by two people, who did manage to live quite independently, there were a few shops nearby for food, etc. I thought they were fabulous, the grounds were laid out with neat flower beds which were looked after by a gardener. Then my Dad turned round and said, "You are not staying here, this is for disabled people and you're not." So, a while ago he had said he didn't want me to join the rat-race because I was fragile — now I wasn't. Again, I was confused and disappointed. Of course, I couldn't stay without my parents' permission as I was under age, 21 was still the age of consent. So I went back to the belief of saying that I didn't want to live away from home and go to college. It was just a dream I guess. So we went back home and my dad was happy,

I was just confused. OK I didn't want to go away to college but I didn't want to be a home-bird either.

I WANTED INDEPENDENCE — a job of my own, wages I could enjoy. Well, it took me six months to persuade Dad that I meant it, so he took me to the youth employment. I really wanted to be a telephonist but they told me I was too short for that job, you had to be five feet two inches minimum. I was just five feet. I decided to take a job in a clothing factory because I was good with a machine and a needle. They sent me to the biggest factory in Leicester at the time because their quota of employing disabled people was bigger than most. I passed the entrance exam and was told to start the following week. It was also where my friend and neighbour Kathleen worked, so we arranged to go to work together, catching the same bus (she always helped me on, it was a good arrangement until she got married and left).

I was filled with dread and excitement all at once as I had been cocooned from what my dad called 'the rat-race', now I was going to join it. I really didn't know what to expect but the supervisor showed me around and introduced me to the girls. She took me to a sewing machine and showed me the job they wanted me to do. It was so simple, all I had to do was sew two ends of elastic together to make a loop and if I could sew 200 dozen a day, I would earn a good wage. She told the truth, it took me a while to get my speed up but I did a minimum of 200 dozen every day and earned a total of £32.00 after tax and insurance, which in those days was very good money.

The girls were great; all seemed very friendly and helpful. I soon got to be special friends with two of them, Linda and Carole. We went around together all the time and soon got the nickname 'The terrible trio'. I don't know why, we never did anything terrible but we did certainly let the world know we were there and made a happy noise when together after work, because we went to the local pubs and had a ball.

Linda and I were only short people but Carole was very tall so we used to walk around arm in arm with Carole in the middle and a shorty either side — it kept us well balanced. Sometimes we would go to each other's homes after work to play records and chat. We always had a good laugh. One day we were in my parents' home when my brother Paul came in. Well, it seemed it was love at first sight for him and Linda. When I got to work the next morning, all Linda could talk about was Paul, and when I got home at night all Paul could talk about was Linda! Carole and I decided to get them together and made arrangements for them to meet and let nature and cupid do the rest, which they did and that was the end of the trio.

Now it was Carole and Carol out for a good time. We carried on going out together (now known as the terrible twins).

Hah! Twins, we definitely were not, but fun we did have in abundance. We even went on holidays together. Carole was a great help to me when I was struggling, like getting on and off buses, or when I fell over, which I did quite often. She would pick me up with ease. I guess because she was so tall it was easier for her to help lift me up and down and then of course, I was very slim.

We often went out on dates with some very nice young men but nothing was ever very serious for either of us. I never thought anyone would ever want to marry me because of my disabilities and Carole never thought anyone would want her because she was so tall, so we just went out for a good time wherever possible.

It was around this time I found out my mum was having an affair with my dad's friend. Apparently, it had been going on for a long time. (I can't say I blamed her really as Dad had treated her badly most of our lives. But having said that, she did goad him on quite a bit and he loved her to distraction. But he seemed to think she was his own private slave and punch-bag, to do his beck-and-call. When he had too much drink, he was very violent towards her). As far as I can see no one should be violent to another. Sometimes he would chase her around the house with the carving knife in his hand. I really don't know what he would have done had he ever caught her (did he ever intend to use it?).

Oh, how I hated these fights. Things came to a head when one day Mum retaliated and punched him back. Wow! She gave him a really good black eye, then she packed her and my youngest brother's bags and left home with him, supposedly to go and live with her lover, who had moved to another town. The trouble was he didn't want to leave his wife and son.

Mum made a life for herself and Michael in Hull. She got a flat and a job near a school for Michael. Carole and I decided to go up and see how she was getting on, we went on the train. Mum kept asking questions about us all at home, she was getting on great but felt guilty about leaving us. Eventually after talking with Dad she decided to come home but only if we moved to another part of town and Dad was to stay off the drink. We begged Mum not to come home because we didn't think Dad would stick to his side of the bargain (can a leopard really change its spots?). We were worried Dad might get back into his bad ways, but she was adamant, she had to come home for ALL her children.

So, it was arranged we would move to the other side of town, our new home was a 3-bed semi, Mum loved it, I hated it. The nearest bus stop was a mile away uphill and to get to work I had to leave even earlier. Mainly, Dad would take me to work though as he had to pass our work to get to his. The bus wasn't too much of a problem going to work, but Dad started work at 7.30 and I started at 8.00 which meant I had to sit around for 40 minutes as I wasn't allowed to start my machine till 8.00.

I was allowed to leave earlier than everyone else too so I didn't get pushed over in the crowds. My baby brother was now going to school in town just up the road from my works, so he would come to the gate to meet me and we would go home together. He too was good at helping me on the bus, no longer a baby but a growing young man.

Paul and Linda came to live with us as she was now pregnant. Mum and Dad turned the dining room into a bedroom for them.

They had a quiet wedding at the registry office, (Paul looked so young in his striped jacket,) so all was going smoothly at home...

...until someone in the street reported Mum and Dad for having too many people living in the house. They were given a choice — send your son and his wife away, or get evicted. It was a no-brainer. Mum wasn't giving in to the council so we ALL had to move out. Her boss had a house to rent and we all moved in there. It was great, a lovely 3-bed detached almost in the town. Paul and Linda finally found a flat just a few streets away.

Carole and I were not seeing as much of each other now as she too had a boyfriend who eventually asked her to marry him. I was so happy for her. She had the fairy-tale wedding and she did look so good in her flowing dress.

Of course, I still went out to parties as I had made a few friends along the way and one time stuck in my mind. I had been out partying with what I thought was a real nice boy and when the party broke up, he took me out into the countryside in his car on a lovely summer night (well actually it was now morning, 4.00am to be precise). When he stopped we got out and went for a walk. Then he made it plain what he really wanted and when I refused he got angry and said if I didn't let him have what he wanted, after all he was entitled after taking me out, — 'Whoa! That's what he thinks!' — then he would leave me here alone. Well, I still refused, so he took off and left me like he said. Now I had no idea where I was, so I walked down this country lane, eventually I ended up at a village called Sharnford. It was one of those cute little places that had about twenty cottages, three pubs and two churches and right there in the middle was a bus stop with a shelter and a seat. I looked at the timetable — it seemed I had one and a half hours before the first bus was due, so I sat and waited. When eventually the bus arrived, I was told I would have a long journey as this bus went to all the villages along the route before going into Leicester. And so we did. I never knew there were so many villages around our city. Some of them were really beautiful but I guess I am a city girl at heart and couldn't wait to get back to my own home. As we didn't have a phone at home I couldn't ring anyone up to say what had happened or where I was.

    My friend Kathleen told me she was going to have a baby. She now lived in a bungalow across town, which made it difficult for me to go see her but we still kept in touch. It was around this time I decided I wanted to learn to drive... BUT... Dad said I would never be able to drive because I wouldn't be able to turn the steering wheel, (he said if I ever wanted to go out he would take me) and I truly think he wanted me to rely on him for the rest of my life. But I didn't agree. Like I have said, I am stubborn. If someone tells me I cannot do something, then I have to try it and find out for myself what I am capable of. So, without telling anyone I went to the British School of Motoring (BSM) talked to the manager, telling him what my disability was like and did he think it was possible for me to learn to drive. He said, "If we get the automatic car and go out for a test drive we will see if you can manage, then we will book you in some lessons, but if you feel you cannot manage, or I feel you're not up to it, then the trial lesson will be free." I agreed and we booked a lesson for the next week.

On the day of my trial lesson, I was once again excited and apprehensive at the same time (what if Dad was right and I couldn't turn the wheels? I would soon find out). We set off, the manager drove us out of town and stopped in a quiet road and said, "Now let's change seats." I looked at him and said, "What? You want me to get behind the wheel now?"

He smiled and said, "Of course, how else will you know if you can do it? Don't worry, it's dual-controlled so we are not in danger." Hmmm. Point taken. With that, I got behind the wheel and never looked back. It was fabulous. I really could do it, once I had gotten used to the width of the car and stopped wavering towards the white line. I found it was so liberating. He asked me to do some parking and practiced going around corners. I managed it all and felt great.

My dad was wrong. The hour seemed to fly by and soon we were back at the driving school where I booked my next lesson. I could only have one lesson a week because the school only had one automatic car between all the BSM offices; they were not too popular in 1969. I didn't tell anyone I was taking driving lessons and booked them for the last hour of work time, telling my boss I had a hospital appointment. So, I always got home at the usual time. Nobody knew until I went home with my pink slip twelve weeks later. All were surprised and pleased for me — except Dad. He just looked at me and said, "You only passed because you're disabled and they had to let a certain quota pass." Thanks Dad. Everyone else congratulated me and gave me some credit for passing first time.

That was a few days before my 21st birthday and there was a big party for me at our local club. It was great, my eldest brother came home with half a dozen of his mates from the ship and I really did have the time of my life. It was then I decided I was going to start having a wild time and go out with as many men as I could but I wanted to do the reverse on them. So, I took the stand to "use 'em and lose 'em," like I had been used for so long. I never thought any man would want me for a wife so I just went out and had as much fun as I could. I even went out with a lesbian and tried that but it definitely didn't do anything for me. Mum said that one day I would 'get into trouble and end up pregnant'. I told her, "Good, then at least I will have someone who loves me for me."

A few weeks before that, I had heard my mum and dad having a heated conversation about me. Mum said, "What are we going to do about Carol? I do not want to be lumbered with her for the rest of my life!"

Well guess what Mum — I have no intention of that happening. Wait until I get my car!

The BSM had also sorted out a car for me to buy during those few weeks and now it was time to go fetch my little

Daffodil (a totally automatic car made by DAF) and get out to do my own thing. I was on a high. I took a few days off work and went driving for miles and miles. Oh, the feeling of total freedom was amazing. The open road and me. Yay!

Now I didn't have to wait around for anyone to pick me up after work. I decided to change jobs and find a smaller place to work — with parking. It was easy in those days to get work; there were more jobs than people, so you had a pick of where you wanted. I actually changed jobs three times in one week because I could. I finally settled into a family business where they started training me as a tailoress, which I found very rewarding although the money was not so good (approximately £11.50 per week). I still earned enough to pay for my car and party a lot, as I had made many new friends. I also found out I loved night driving, it was so different from daytime. For a start, there was NO traffic and being enveloped in darkness, it was like being in a different world. Sometimes my youngest brother asked if he could come along too, he was always quiet so I said OK. We would go for miles down little country roads that I didn't have a clue where we were or where we would end up.

I think we were both amazed at how much wildlife there is out there and I think I always thought animals were kept inside at night (typical city girl attitude!). One night we were going down a twisty little road, my headlights were on main beam, it was pitch black all around. Suddenly there in front of us were lots of glowing green eyes! I wondered what on earth we were heading into, it looked really spooky. As we came up to a T-junction my lights caught some of their bodies too, it was a flock of sheep. Phew! That felt scary but we had to laugh when we realised how silly we had been.

We were still giggling about it when we got home, oh BIG mistake. It woke mother up. She said, "What are you doing up at this time of the morning?" I said we have just been for a drive;

she looked straight at me and replied. "I would appreciate it if you didn't keep your brother out till 2.00am; he has to get up for school tomorrow." With that, she stormed off back to bed. We still went out but kept very quiet when coming home.

I went to visit Kathleen with her new family, her husband had bought a boat, (Harold called it a cruiser) for the rivers around where they lived. Sometimes I would go out with them for a weekend, travelling along some lovely peaceful and beautiful places. I never realised there was so much tranquillity in the countryside. Though it was peaceful, it certainly wasn't quiet, with all the birds singing, bees buzzing, cattle calling, ducks quacking, etc., but they were all gentle noises and sort of blended into the surroundings so nothing overwhelmed you. It was like being in a different world and I loved it.

I even got to steer the boat sometimes. The first time I said to Harold, "People on the water are so friendly — they keep waving at me." He replied, "Maybe it's because you're on the wrong side of the river," and smiled. That's when I learned that boats steer on the opposite side of the river as cars on the road. It felt strange doing that but it was fabulous.

They were such magical times but of course, all good things come to an end and so it did when they decided to move away from Leicester to live in Mablethorpe - 120 miles away.

I sometimes went to the local pub with Mum and Dad on a Friday evening and on one of these times, Dad started talking to a really good-looking young man. Dad brought him over and we got talking, his name was Roy. It seemed we had a lot in common and we chatted most of the evening. When it was near time to go he asked if he could see me again. Well of course I said yes and we arranged to meet two days later. He was working all weekend; he was a policeman and did shifts.

That was the start of a wonderful relationship. He came to the house to pick me up, and sometimes he came in the Panda car (you can bet that got the neighbours talking). He often came round for tea, Mum and Dad thought he was fabulous, more like hoping that we'd get married. Well, funnily enough, Roy did ask me to marry him. I think Mum and Dad were more happy than me, as Roy would tell them how much he was going to make my life as easy as possible and wait on me hand and foot. They just lapped it up, and so it began — wedding plans. We went to the vicar next door and booked the wedding for July, it was now May. Roy said he didn't want to wait any longer than that, so the Reverend got the papers and we filled them all in. He told us the Banns would be read three weeks before the wedding.

Now I heard a saying that the biggest villains are the police themselves, I never believed that until now. One day Roy never turned up for our date and as we didn't have a telephone, he couldn't ring me up to tell me why. So, I went to the phone box and rang the police station, they told me he was on the sick but wouldn't tell me where he lived. It was then I realised how little I know about Roy and his life. I went back home and told Mum he was sick, which is when she remembered he told her he was living in a police house on New Parks Estate. There weren't many of them around there so Dad took me and he knocked on a door and asked the person if they knew which house Roy lived in, they told us just two doors down.

I went and knocked on the door. Roy answered looking really sick when he saw me. Then a woman behind him said, "Who's this Roy, your little bit on the side?" She told me to go if I knew what was good for me. Roy said he would come round soon and explain.

I had to wait three days before he was 'well enough'. He told me he was really sorry but he was already married and that was his wife at the door. Apparently, she was Maltese and had been back home in Malta visiting her family. I had been a distraction that got out of hand, while she was away. He wanted me to forgive him because he really had fallen in love with me but marriage was a pipe dream as they were both Catholic so would never divorce.

I was completely devastated and felt so foolish that I had believed in him so much and after cancelling the wedding, I went into a depression, crying, and hating all men as low-life scum, vowing I would never let myself fall again. But once I began to get out and about, I did what I usually do and picked myself up, dusted myself down and got back in the social scene, sticking to a group sooner than singles. I went to some really wild parties and had a great time, sometimes we partied all night. A few times the police were called to shut us up, so we would get into vehicles and go racing down the motorway at 2-3 am and go join another party — life became hectic and — hollow.

I started staying home more and reading and playing my records. I had a big collection and could play songs for weeks without repeating any. After a few weeks of me staying home Mum was once again worried she would be stuck with me forever and unknown to me, she had placed an advert in the 'friendships wanted' part of our local newspaper. Only when the answers started coming in did she tell me about it. She gave me a big bundle of letters and asked me to at least look at them. I did and was amazed at how many lonely people there were, also how many of them I actually knew.

So, I got to thinking, this could be kind of fun and started taking a better look at them. I filtered out all the ones I knew and the ones that sounded nuts (yes, there were plenty of them) and also the ones who admitted to being married whose wives didn't understand them. Duh. I wonder why!

I wrote to ones that sounded okay and were around my age, always agreeing to meet them in a public place and always where I could see them before they saw me, so if I didn't like the look of 'em I was off! My evenings were busy dating these lonely men, but I never went out with one more than once. None seemed to have the "WOW" factor; most were pleasant and well-mannered but there were a few who wanted payment of sex at the end of the evening for 'buying me drinks and a meal.' They told me it was their right. Some men will always be animals, I suppose.

So, when I met Tony for the first time I was amazed how well we got on and how much we had in common, like our tastes in music, food, drinks, films etc. I also told him about my disability — although I didn't look like there was anything wrong there were many things I couldn't do — he said that was not a problem for him. For the first time in months I didn't want the night to end. Of course, it had to, but we made a date for Saturday - hmmm — two days away. Tony had told me he was just out of the army after serving nine years and was at the moment without a job. Being away from home for so long he had lost contact with all his friends and was seeking new ones, hence the letter and our meeting. Our second date was even better than the first. He was so considerate and kind, and oh, SOOOOO SEXY! My insides turned to mush every time I looked at him (I found out later on that he felt the same). After that evening, we saw each other every evening.

We went to a night club to dance, which of course I couldn't do apart from the slow ones, but I loved to watch the couples swishing around the floor. One night I was wearing a psychedelic full circle dress and as I sat there watching the others, I said I wish I could swirl my dress like that and Tony said, "You can. Come on." He got up and took my hand, I pulled back and said, "You know I can't," he said, "Trust me you will." I went onto the dance floor and we started to sway then he told me to stand on his feet (I thought he had gone nutty or something). He saw me hesitate and said again, "Trust me and hold on." So, I did and sure enough he whizzed me around that dance floor and my skirt flew out and I felt wonderful. I hadn't noticed most people had left the floor and were watching us and when we stopped they all applauded us... It was wonderful. Most mornings I got home from being with Tony at 3am having to get up for work at 6.30am. I wonder where all the energy came from. After three weeks, I was taking days off to be with him and he proposed to me while we were on the Bradgate Park. That threw me and all my doubts came flooding back, so I said I would have to think about it. I thought he can't mean it; he must be having a laugh so I said no. He asked me why. First, I said, "What will your parents think marrying a disabled girl?" to which he replied:

"One: Your disability doesn't disturb me. Just because you can't do some things so-called 'normal' people can, does not make you a lesser person. Two: It will be me marrying you, not my parents!"

So then, I told him about Roy and the wedding that never was. It took Tony a while but he convinced me that he would never do to me what others had. He respected and loved me and wanted to spend the rest of his life with me. So, I said yes. Best decision I ever made.

And so it began again — wedding plans. I would have been happy with a Register Office wedding but Tony said it's a church one or nothing. So we went back to the vicar and told him we would like to get married in his church. The first thing he said while looking at me was, "I hope this one's not married too." Duh! It's a good job I had told Tony about Roy.

We arranged for the parents to all meet and discuss what we wanted over a meal. When our mums heard which church we were using they both said at the same time, "That's the one I got married in!" Spooky! I never knew that until then. I only chose that church because we lived next door and I did go occasionally.

When they started talking about having the choir and flowers and photos and bridesmaids, sit-down, or buffet-meals, how many guests? Did you know that church has the longest aisle in Leicester? Etc., etc. I nearly blew my top. I didn't want lots of fuss - just a quiet wedding would do, so we compromised. A small wedding with no more than fifty people, a sit-down meal in the afternoon and meet up at the Egyptian Queen for the youngsters, as this pub had a good disco.

Preparing for a wedding is a very stressful time and I can understand why they say, "The bride looks so happy" — that's because **she is so relieved at last all the sorting out and getting prepared is finally OVER!**

Having made my bridesmaid dresses myself didn't help the stress levels, after all there was only three of them, but I could do it and it did save lots of money, which we would need to start our home up.

And so, on January 23rd, 1971 at 12:30 pm we were wed, photos were taken and then we went out of town for the festivities. We had arranged for a sit-down meal for all and it was great, we sat in a U-shape with us at the head of the table. I felt so special, everyone was smiling and saying nice things. When they brought the cake in it looked fab. Only two tiers but I was told to save the top layer for the next event (I wasn't sure what they meant but did so anyway). After that we went home to change then we all went to a pub for a disco where we danced for hours. When Tony and I stood up to go the band started to play something and the leader said over the mike, **"There go the honeymooners and we know what they will be getting up to,"** to which everyone clapped and cheered and I went bright red and smiled. We left them all to carry on their merriment — and a good time was had by all.

Our First Home

Our first home was a three-bedroomed terrace near to town so most shops were within walking distance. Tony used all his severance pay from the army to put down a deposit. We decided to spend our honeymoon in our new home, where I had my first revelation. As you may have gathered from earlier — I didn't rate sex much. It seemed all men thought we were there for was for them to release their frustrations and I honestly thought that hard thing between their legs was a BONE! Oh, what a silly, naive person I had been. Well, all that changed on our honeymoon. Tony was the perfect gentleman and put my pleasures first, trouble was I didn't know much about pleasure, I didn't think I deserved any. So he had his work cut out for him. Well, he succeeded, in the two weeks we had in our love-nest, I turned from a wilting flower to being **insatiable**! I had never experienced such pleasure; it was like going into a darkened room and pulling the curtains open to a bright, sunny day. EVERYTHING WAS SO DIFFERENT - colours, sound, touch, and smell - I felt different too. Gosh, I felt like I could do **ANYTHING.**

It was very strange being a wife, kind of nice, but I had so much to learn as I had to learn to cook, clean, food shop wisely. That was fun. I didn't have a clue about veggies, meat, etc., what to buy or how to cook it. Oh, joy. But of course Tony was in the same position, so we learnt stuff together. I left the finances to Tony because maths was never a strong subject for me, (on reflection now, that is a big mistake, all couples should know how to balance the books) but we were young and had a lot to learn. I got lucky with the food and veg, there were two corner shops very near, both had understanding of the newly-weds and were always ready to give advice on what to buy and how to cook it and the butcher went to the effort of boning our meat as well as advising me the best way to cook it.

People were so much more helpful in those early days. *I must admit I found it quite a struggle running a home and going out to work full time, but Tony knew how to unwind me in the evenings. When our chores were finished, I would sit on the floor in front of him and he would spend ages brushing my hair, which was quite long again. I found it really relaxing and apparently Tony enjoyed it too.

Tony was now working in the taxation department, for the grand wage of £8.50 per week — 9-5. When he had finished in the office he came home and did the cleaning while I cooked the dinner. I was still working and finished an hour before Tony, so I shopped for the food, before going home to cook. We didn't have a fridge so had to shop every day. Our milk was kept cool in a bucket of water in the kitchen.

The Government had just changed our money over from pounds, shillings and pence to decimal, this too, I found hard to come to terms with. Guess I was never any good at changes. I was always happy with what I knew but of course nothing stays the same and I had to learn to adapt like everyone else.

Being married didn't stop us having fun either. We still went out to parties and at least once a month we would have one at our home (bring your own bottle type, so it wasn't expensive). We invited the neighbours too so they didn't worry about any noise.

After a few weeks of marriage I started to feel ill. We found out I was pregnant, something neither of us had talked about before and I don't know how I really felt about it. We didn't tell anyone about it, as it was still early. We said we would wait a few more weeks before announcing it, but Mother Nature had different plans and after a short while I had a miscarriage and had to be taken into hospital. After having a D&C and many examinations the doctors all came to the same conclusion — because of my weakness it was doubtful I would ever be able to carry a baby to full term. That was a bit of a blow and the usual thing happened that always does with me — when I am told I cannot do something because of my disability, for **some strange reason, I have to prove them wrong**. I don't really understand myself sometimes but I always react the same way.

So I became obsessed with becoming pregnant again and shortly after my 23rd year on this earth, I got my wish. I was again pregnant, this time the doctor said I was to have a dose of injections to help strengthen my muscles (I guess it must have been some steroid). Every time he gave me one of these injections I fainted. The doctor was really surprised and said, "That is not supposed to happen."

Around the fourth month we told our parents they were going to be grandparents. My dad hit the panic button and asked how on earth was I going manage? Then he got the shingles that lasted through until our baby was born. Then they went away as quick as they had come up. Amazing!

I also had to sell my car when I had to stop working because we just could not afford the repayments. Selling it was the obvious thing to do. I watched as it was driven away and cried my eyes out!

Beginning the eighth month, I read a book on having a baby and I saw a picture of where the baby comes out when we go into labour. Well, then I hit the panic button. I sat there and cried, telling Tony I couldn't go through with it. He said, "Well how did you think the baby was coming out?" and, "It's too late to worry about it now." Just goes to show how naive I still was.

Finally came the time when our beautiful daughter was born. The labour only lasted two and half hours. She weighed in at six pounds, seven ounces on April 19, 1972, at 1:20 pm. She looked so tiny and fragile and suddenly I realised I was going to be in charge of a tiny human being. How on earth was I going to manage? I don't think I had ever given it any thought before. This tiny human being, was relying upon us to look after and love and care for her well-being. I must admit I panicked a little and said to Tony's mum "What shall I do? Will I really be able to cope, as she got bigger and heavier, the most I can pick up is 12 pounds, what do I do when she exceeds that?" She replied, "Don't worry, the baby will understand and know what you can and cannot do, she will help you." I said, "How can she possibly do that? She is a tiny baby." Mum replied, "She just will, trust me."

Strangely enough she really did, she was helping me to dress her, pushing her arms through sleeves and she looked at me as if to say, 'Don't worry Mum, we will be fine together.' It was a very strange experience, at six weeks she was trying to stay sitting up on her own, which apparently is unheard of. It didn't take her long, it seems she is as determined as her mum!

The times when Tony was at work were the hardest. I had to feed, wash and dress her and change her nappies (these were the terry nappies fastened with pins, not the disposable kind they have now) while she lay in the pram where Tony put her before going to work. She was really good and never seemed distressed. I couldn't breast feed her for the same reason, no one ever told me about expressing my milk. They just said, "If you're not going to breast feed — here take this" and gave me a little blue pill which apparently dries up the milk. I just didn't have the strength to hold her for long enough, so I put a chair by the pram and fed her a bottle then winded her in there too. Then while she had a sleep I would get on with washing her nappies and clothes all by hand as we still didn't have a washing-machine or dryer. Such fun times!

The health visitors were not happy with me doing things unconventionally and when Colette stood up on her own at six months they were furious, saying I had forced her and that she would grow up with terribly bowed legs. According to them, no baby should be even sitting up, let alone standing on their own at that age. We did in fact try and stop her from getting up but she was a very determined baby (well years later let me tell you, now, she has **FABULOUS LEGS** not a bow in sight). It just goes to show how much these so- called experts really know! Our daughter seemed to be a strong and healthy child and there were no signs of my disability. She grew very quickly and was able to understand things very well. She also enjoyed our parties and was "The Belle of the Ball!"

As I could no longer go out to work, I got a job working at home, with a knitwear company sewing zips on cardigans. It was very tedious but the pay was good. They supplied the machine, brought the work to me, and came to pick it up when I had finished.

So our days were pretty full and things seemed to be ticking along nicely, until we started noticing more and more coloured people living in our street. One day, the Immigration Office and the Police performed a raid and found over 200 people living in the attics of all the houses on one side of the street (that was a complete row of 35 terraced houses). One of the owners had let his relatives in his home, then they went up into the attic and made holes in the adjoining walls all the way down the row. It was only when someone further along heard noises in their attic and thought it was rats so they called the vermin controllers out, who then reported to the immigration.

There was a lot of unrest and groups of foreigners walked around in gangs making life very unpleasant for all. I personally felt very vulnerable when out with Colette and got more nervous as the troubles worsened, so in the end we decided to sell up and go elsewhere. As you can imagine our home sold very quickly (it was only foreigners showing interest). We found a lovely bungalow just out of town. My boss said he would still bring me work over, so everything should have been great, but of course it wasn't, because after the first few visits with the work, my boss said it was too far for him to bring it out, so he came and took the machine and that was that.

The big problem was we had taken my wages into account when having to pay the mortgage. That was a mistake. I tried to get another job but there wasn't much call for home workers on this side of town apparently.

Then Tony started feeling ill, he was getting lots of pain in his arm and found it really difficult to move it. He went to the docs a few times and each time was told there was nothing wrong, so now Tony was on sick pay and I was out of work. There was not enough money to cover everything and for a few weeks Tony and I basically lived on bread and jam or baked beans. We made sure Colette had proper meals but that was it... until my mum found out. Then she started to bring us food over. As she worked in a grocery shop she brought all the special offers, so we had some variety to our diet.

It wasn't enough though and after a lot of discussion we decided to sell up and buy a mobile home, that way we would no longer need a mortgage, which sounded good. Although there are many mobile home sites, there are not many that allow children.

We finally found one in Lincolnshire, a little place called Welton. With the money (£1,950) we had left over from the sale of the bungalow we bought it —a three bedroomed mobile home with full central heating completely furnished, and the only things we had to take were our personal stuff.

The Park manager arranged to have a set of smaller shallow steps made so it was easier for me to get in and out of the home. Here at least our life would be easier to manage and now we no longer had a mortgage we could relax a little. We even went to the expense of buying a little washing machine and separate spin-dryer, at least we wouldn't have to wash the nappies or the bed sheets and towels by hand any more. Oh, such luxury.

However, Tony's arm started to really hurt. He went to the hospital yet again and yet again they told him there was nothing wrong. When he came home he just sat down and cried, because the pain was so bad. This really did worry me because I had never seen him cry before so I knew he must be in agony. I felt so helpless. There was nothing I could do but give him paracetamol for the pain. Eventually he told me the hospital had told him he would be better off to have his arm removed, and should see a psychiatrist as all the pain was in his mind — which I find ridiculous when they said there was nothing wrong. No, he would never agree to that, so with no help coming forward we just soldiered on, making sure we had a good supply of paracetamol, what other choice did we have?

Summer came and all seemed right with the world. Our home was very nice and easy to look after, Tony's arm seemed to be less painful and we had made some very good friends. One lady in particular whose name was Winnie looked after Colette quite a bit for us. Living on a mobile home park is good from the safety angle, the people were all so friendly. There was no traffic and it was very quiet so Colette was safe to be out but Winnie always kept an eye on her.

Tony had another job working in the dairy doing their books. While he was at work I was supposed to be looking after Colette who was now a 13-month-old and a little mischief. She knew I couldn't catch her when she ran but Winnie was always nearby and she did catch her, thank goodness for friends. The summer seemed to fly, by the end August I started to feel ill and after going to the doctors we found out I was pregnant again. I wasn't sure how I felt about this, after all I had proved I could do it already. I also dreaded telling my dad as he had been so ill last time, but all he said was, "It's OK, I know you can do it now so I won't worry." Tony, however, was excited. He was hoping for a boy. I became more and more ill, and lost three stone in weight. I could not keep anything down apart from yoghurt. With Tony working in the dairy I was able to have lots of yoghurt.

Thank goodness we have some good neighbours because I spent more time laying down than looking after our home and child. Winnie often cooked for us even though she had five children of her own. She was a little bundle of dynamite!

It's very strange how things go in cycles. We had a marvellous summer, now things seemed to be going wrong. Apart from my feeling ill, Tony's arm started to play up again and he was taking more time off work. Then he lost his job, we needed more help and after talking to parents we decided it was time to go back to Leicester. Tony's mum and dad said we could stay with them until we found a place of our own. That is just what we did, we put the mobile home up for sale and went to live with Tony's mum and dad. Apparently they had been missing us a lot.

Tony had managed to get an office job just a half mile up the road; he bought a bicycle so getting there and back was no problem. It was not always easy living with in-laws. They were, on the whole, very accommodating considering their home had been invaded. In fact there were only two bad incidents that I remember. Tony's dad got upset when we had been there three months. He had been on nightshift and got upset because he couldn't sleep "with a noisy kid," (Colette) and was dreading we would still be there when the baby was born and "screaming the place down." Tony's mum got very upset when the unborn baby kicked a cup of tea on her brand-new carpet! My fault I had gotten into the habit of resting my cup on my very large tummy and I had a very active baby in there! Of course, I did try and keep Colette entertained while her Daddy was at work but it was difficult being pregnant and this time I was SO BIG, completely the opposite to when I carried Colette.

We did everything we could to get out of there as fast as we could because we too wanted our own space back. We eventually found a cottage we could afford just two miles up the road. Finally, we signed the papers. The moving in date was set. I went into labour two days before moving in, after being induced, because both the baby and I were having problems. The labour was very long and painful. After ten hours, the doctor said I would have to have a caesarean if the baby wasn't born in the next hour.

Well thank goodness, he was born 25 minutes later. They took him away and I didn't see him for three days. I was told it was because I needed a rest before my operation, I was going to be sterilised because I didn't want to go through this EVER AGAIN. I didn't think I could have managed to look after any more children, in fact I was really worried about HOW I was going to cope with two children.

I had to stay in hospital for two weeks because of the sterilisation operation — which was scary because I woke up in the middle of the procedure! I saw the big bright light over us and heard the doctors talking. I could feel them prodding and pulling my insides about. Then someone noticed I was awake and trying to swallow BUT I had something down my throat holding my tongue down so I couldn't swallow and I was panicking. Then a mask went over my face and I remember no more.

After having a baby there are certain exercises to do to get your body back in shape. Unfortunately, I couldn't do most of them, not knowing at that time that I had MITO. Not knowing I was exercise intolerant, I became very frustrated wondering where and how I was going wrong. Now years later I finally understand my problems.

During that time, Tony and Colette moved into our little cottage and got everything ready for me and Jason to join them. It was so nice to be in our own home again, I was very grateful to Tony's parents for putting up with us all but so relieved to be on our own again.

If I thought I was going to cope with my new baby as I had before, I soon found out how wrong I was. Although I still had to feed, clothe etc., in the pram, Jason had other ideas about leaving him alone. He would yell the place down if I wasn't in sight, so looking after Colette too was very difficult. Of course, she was now two years old going on 22 and did help an awful lot fetching stuff to help her brother. Sometimes she would even rock him to sleep in the pram.

And so, our life settled down for a while. I even felt good enough to offer help to Tony's sister. She needed someone to look after her two children during the long summer holiday. I volunteered, as they were good kids and a little older than ours so I knew they would be OK, in fact they helped me lots. They managed to keep Colette happy while I was seeing to Jason and we all sat down to a good meal each day, so they were clean and fed when their mum came to fetch them home each night. The summer came and went without any traumas.

One day a lady from the social services came around to see how I was coping. It seemed she was worried about the children not getting out. I pointed out to her that there was no chance of me managing both the children on to a bus when I couldn't even get myself on one. She suggested I get a car as they knew I could drive. I told her I would love one but could not afford it. She then told me there was a new scheme just started up called Motability, specially for disabled people to claim, to get them out and about. She gave me all the forms and left it up to us to claim or not. When Tony came home from work, we filled them in and he posted them. A few weeks later, we had a reply, saying that I had to go to Nottingham for an ability test. If I passed, I could have a car.

After making arrangements for the children to be looked after and for my dad to take me, I had a medical first. They wanted to know all about my disability and what it was. Of course, we still didn't know then. It was still some sort of Muscular Dystrophy is all we knew. I passed all the tests but the last one, which was:

I had to sit behind the wheel of an old Rover with flat tyres and turn the wheel as if I was going round a corner. Well, of course, I couldn't do it. I told them the test was totally unfair. They said, "Of course it's not, you will have to go around corners when driving." I replied, "YES that is true but not with flat tyres I won't," but they didn't agree and failed me. I went home in tears.

Tony on the other hand was furious, he got straight on to our local MP and told him what a shambles he thought the test was. The MP was very helpful and advised me to go to a reputable driving school and ask for a lesson to see if indeed I was unable to handle a car. Which is what I did. I went back to the BSM and told them what had happened and asked if I could book just one lesson to be evaluated on my competence. The strange thing was the manager who took me out for my very first lesson remembered me and he personally took me out for an hour, refused any payment because he said I was still a very competent driver, and had no hesitation in saying so. I still have the letter he wrote.

So, with the help of some caring people I had a car delivered to our home a couple of weeks later. Now I really could get out and about with the children! As I have said before getting a smaller car with an automatic gearbox was not easy in those days but they brought me this little Mini, which was great. We went out nearly every day. Of course, there were no seat belts in those days either, so keeping two little ones still whilst driving was sometimes challenging, but on the whole our kids did sit still when I told them to.

The time flew by, we seemed to be settled. Tony's job was going well and his arm only niggled him from time to time. The children were going out with me in the car a few days a week. Colette was going to play-school each morning, a neighbour took her and brought her home for me, which was very nice of her. She said she understood about disability because her daughter was disabled with autism and took a lot of handling.

It was then we realised Colette had developed a squint and it was a lot worse when she was tired. We took her to the doctor who said we had to be referred to the hospital. There were many visits. She ended up having to wear glasses with a patch on to strengthen one eye as it was weaker than the other. After a few months, they said she would have to have an operation. If the surgery was successful she would no longer need the glasses. All this was very stressful as Colette also had an inborn fear of MEN, she was fine talking to them but she would never let any man touch her but her dad; no granddads, uncles, cousins or friends could even put a hand on her before she would yell the place down. We being there had always managed to keep her calm but the hospital visit meant she had to go in an ambulance for a transfer to another and so the ambulance man picked her up to put her inside.

Well, she did her usual and screamed the place down all the time, kicking him too and boy did she have a strong kick. The poor man was bewildered. He said, "I never did anything to her." After everyone had calmed down I explained her fear. I don't know where it had come from but it seems she had always had it. It was not that she was shy, as she like her mum would talk to anyone anytime and be mischievous, she just couldn't stand being touched by men.

My disability was still the about the same. I didn't give it much thought either as Tony and I had worked out a routine to get the kids sorted before he went to work. Once he had brought Jason downstairs and put him in the pram I just followed on as I had before. The only problem really was, Jason didn't want to move as Colette had. It did worry me, but he seemed OK. When the social came to check on us she said he probably wasn't moving much because he was so big. She said I was feeding him too much and if I cut his food down a little he would soon be on the move. The trouble was he didn't eat much, he refused most solid meals. All he wanted was milk. He drank two bottles at each meal. He certainly didn't sleep much. He never had an afternoon nap.

One day when the children were a little older I decided to take them to the cinema to watch the Walt Disney film Bambi. All was well until trying to get into our seats Colette stumbled in the dark. A kind young man said, "Come here love, let me help," and before I realised what he was doing he picked her up to pass her over the seats. Well, that was it, she let out the loudest scream you ever heard. The man dropped her, she fell on the floor and everyone turned around to see what was going on. Well, I just got hold of her and Jason and left. It was all too much. I just drove us back home and never tried to take them anywhere in a public place on my own ever again. To this day Colette still refuses to watch that film.

I had to entertain Jason more than I did with Colette. I had also been back to my old boss and asked him for outwork now we lived nearer. He was more than happy to supply me with a machine and work. Now we would have some spending money.

I had to do my outwork when the children had gone to bed and didn't usually finish until midnight. Again, I wonder where I got all that energy from (must be the reason most people have children while they are young because their energy levels are better).

The cottage we were living in was a row of four and our neighbours were very friendly. The one we shared the entry with was called Wilfred. He was old and had lived there all his life. We asked him if he minded us fencing off our garden as it was all open at the time, when we said it was to keep the children in, as there was a main road on the front and also to keep them off his garden, which he took great pride in. He actually helped

Tony to build it, so now at least I could let them out in the garden when it was dry and know they were safe. I still I did most my work during the evening but sometimes I would do some while they were playing.

One day Wilf came knocking on the door, blood was streaming from his face. He was holding a cloth up to his nose, he wanted to know if I could help him to stop the bleeding. I tried but nothing seemed to work so I told him I would take him into town to hospital. We got the kids in the back and off we went. Unfortunately, he never came back. Apparently, he was riddled with cancer and his veins kept bursting. It was very strange without Wilf next door. His garden became overgrown and his son only came to tidy it up once he had sold the cottage.

I seemed to be spending a lot of time at the hospital as they had finally found out what was wrong with Tony's arm. It wasn't all in his mind. He actually had osteomyelitis in the bone and fortunately for us the young doctor who found it actually had the courage to override the consultant, who still told Tony there was nothing wrong.

The consultant told this young upstart to, "Go ahead, do the tests and make a fool of yourself, then you will apologise."

Well, thank goodness he did lots of tests and sure enough found a tiny hairline crack in Tony's bone. When they opened up Tony's arm the consultant found so much poison in there, he said Tony would have died within two weeks. They actually drained two and a half pints of poison out of Tony's body, most of his muscle had to be cut away and the bad bone was removed to be replaced by some sort of plastic bone. At least all this meant he didn't have to have his arm removed but he did have to build the remaining muscle back up, which took many months. The scar goes from the top of his arm, twists around the back, and stops at the elbow. Even with his arm in a sling he still managed to help look after the children when he got out of the hospital. After we got over the shock of realising how near we were to losing him it was so good knowing there really had been something wrong. Now the pain was gone, apart from the scar wound, but that would soon heal.

At this time, we were thinking of moving as Tony's mum had said there was a house for sale in the next street from her and around the corner from Tony's sister. It was much nearer to his work which, after having a few weeks off was getting near to time for him to get back, so logically it would make more sense to move there and be near to more help. It was a three-bedroomed semi, a repossession house and was selling for a third of the price, all the mortgage people wanted was their money back. We did manage to purchase it. So here we were yet again packing up and moving. Here's hoping this time will be the last!

So now we have this fine modern house, the children have a bedroom each, there is a dining area too, giving us twice as much room as we had in the cottage. The garden was also very big and it was fenced off so the children could play in the back without me having to worry about them much. Tony's parents lived down the next street, his sister around the corner and one of my brothers bought a house on our street too, so there were lots of family nearby. Now it was winter, we had settled down nicely. The children still played in the garden when it was dry and I was still doing my out working. The only difference with that was now I had a car I could take the work back when I had finished it, so I didn't have to rely on my boss to come and bring me more when he had the time.

One day it started snowing so hard it was building up against our back door which was mainly one sheet of fluted glass. With the weight of snow that was hitting it, there was a sudden crash and the whole door crashed in and snow started piling up in the kitchen. It was freezing, I was terrified, Tony was at work, so I called his dad and asked if he could come over, which he did. He got a sheet of plywood from his shed (he was a carpenter) and screwed it up as a temporary fix. We had to get a new back door but didn't make the mistake of buying a flutter glass one. No, we bought a good solid wooden one; we didn't want to go through that again.

Tony and I had never had such a big garden before nor had we ever grown anything for ourselves, so in the spring we thought we would give it a go and started to grow our own veggies and salads, which were growing nicely, until. Would you believe it — after the worst winter ever the spring was really dry and that was the year of the drought (1976). We were told not to use any water we didn't need and to only put three inches in our baths and share as much as possible. If the situation were to worsen, the authorities would have to install stand pipes, which after a few weeks they did. The only water we could have, we had to go out into the street and queue, to fill our containers, so there was none for the new plants we had put in the garden and they all died.

On top of that Tony was having trouble with his arm again. They discovered one of the stitches had gone inwards and had festered. He had to have more time off work, a nurse came in every day to drain out the stuff and put clean dressings on.

While he was away, his office transferred to the city, so when he was ready to go back to work he now had to get the train into town instead of going a few streets away. Well all this became too much as he was having to leave early and get home late (the trains didn't run more than one every couple of hours). If he missed one the wait was long for the next and he was worried about leaving me and the children for so long, even though there were plenty of family around. We preferred to work as a team and not rely on others too much, so, it was time to move into the city where the work was easier to get to.

Tony's mum hated the idea and when she saw the terraced house we were going to buy she said, "I'll give you six months here before you are wanting to move back out of town," (she was kind of a snob in as much as terraced houses were the lowest place to live) but to be honest, Tony and I prefer them and we loved living so near to all the shops, banks etc. There was a fabulous park just a few minutes away, the school was only around the corner and my mum and dad lived just down the road. As was Tony's work, so for us there was no contest, this would do us nicely for a few years.

And so here we are in our terraced house. It's June 1977, the "Silver Jubilee Year" for the Queen and Philip. It is another hot summer and the children are still parading around naked and waving their little flags (oh, to be so young and carefree).

Tony now only has to walk a couple of streets to work. We have got Colette into the local school, much to her disgust (she has inherited my hatred of schools). Whereas Jason really would love to go, he has to wait another year because he is too young, although if we are lucky and there is a space, he may be able to go part time in six months.

During the long summer holidays my children still had to do some schoolwork. I would set them maths and spelling tests that were fun as well as practical, partly to help them to learn but also to help pass some time together as I refused to let them play out in the streets where I couldn't keep my eye on them. It was great living so near to the shops, we would walk to them me in the middle and a child holding each hand. We also went over to the park to feed the ducks. I took them in the car to visit other relations (and there were MANY). We would get home and prepare the meal together too, so it was ready when Tony came home from work. All in all, life was good.

There was a big dull concrete covered wall opposite the kitchen window and I said to Tony, "Shame we can't brighten that up a bit." He said, "We can." Then he went and got the kids poster paints and painted some lovely flowers on there. We both thought they would wash off when the rains came, but they didn't, they lasted for years.

When Jason was old enough to go to school, I decided I wanted to go back to work. I went and signed up with an agency to do some part time temporary office work and a mother whose children went to the same school looked after Colette and Jason for the last hour before I came home. Tony also wanted a change and the opportunity came up for him to go back to college taking a course on Accounting and Company Law. Living this close to the town was so much easier as the college too was only a short walk away; he managed to get a grant, so though things would be tight we should manage money wise. The course was an intensive one for a year only. It really was hard work for Tony though, as he had to study for long hours and he still had to help me around the house with the children. To be honest now they were a bit older it wasn't too hard to look after them. They actually wanted to look after ME and were always looking out so I didn't fall or trip over anything. Tony's mum's words often came back to me, **"They will know and understand."** Well, they sure did seem to, all the time they were growing up, they never once complained because I couldn't play on the floor with them as their dad did. I was okay to read and play board games with, etc., but no rough and tumble. They took it all in their stride. I was indeed TRULY BLESSED to have such good kids.

Although there was one frustrating thing I was having trouble with and that was Jason's eye problem. He only had 20% vision in one eye and he was supposed to wear glasses with a patch on to strengthen it. But would he wear them? Would he heck! How do you tell a young child it's for his own good and one day it will make his eye better? I even took desperate measures. One night coming back from visiting Tony's parents, as we were driving through the dark country lanes, I parked the car and switched the lights off. Well, it really was pitch black, even I felt scared. The kids said, "Why have we stopped here Mum? Please put the lights on." I said to Jason, "Do you like this darkness?" He said he didn't, it scared him and could we have the lights on and I replied, "Well, this is how it is when you're blind and if you don't wear your patch this is what it could be like for you forever." He started crying and said, "Okay, I will wear it, put the lights on." My victory was short-lived. As soon as he was home he said, "I won't wear my glasses ever." And he never did.

As the time passed by it became more difficult to manage the finances. The cost of living was rising faster than my wages as I was still only working part time. I decided to look for a full-time job, but I really needed something in the evenings so I could still be home with the children when they get home from school. I wanted to get away from sewing machines and do something else. I scoured the newspaper every day and finally found the perfect position. The ad read "NIGHT OWLS WANTED" and it was for the job I had always wanted to do — to be a telephonist. They had lowered the height restriction. BT wanted people to work the twilight shift with one or two full nights and the pay they were offering was more than I would have dreamed of, so I applied. I got a reply two weeks later asking me to go for an interview. I went and passed and was told they would take me in the next training period which was in September and if I passed the ten-week course the job would be mine.

So now it was near the end of June, Tony's course was nearly at an end, depending on his exam results (which he would know at the end of August); he had the offer of a couple of jobs. Now all we had to do was struggle on for a few more months. We decided to go to our bank manager and ask him if he would let us have an overdraft if things got too bad. He looked at us and smiling said, "Let me get this right, neither of you are working yet you want me to lend you money?" We said, "Yes, basically. We have jobs to start in three months, so this is just temporary." We showed him our letters from the companies promising the jobs. He read them and gave us a funny look then said, "It is not something we would normally do but under the circumstances I will allow you an overdraft of £250.00. Do not let me down and abuse it." Well, we said we wouldn't and were hoping not to use it at all, but wanted a safety net in case something came up. As it happened, we did use it a couple of times but for small amounts that we could easily pay back.

As always seems to happen with us, when a really important time approaches, trouble comes hot on its tail. This time it was when Tony was taking his exams. He got the flu. Oh, joy! He only had one chance at these exams so he had to take them. He took as much medication as was possible without dulling his mind completely (Accounting and Company Law I had learnt over the last few months can be VERY BORING). The exams took three days. Tony did his best. Now we had to wait a while for the results. While we waited, we enjoyed the remaining summer holidays the children had from school. We had lots of hazy, crazy days going on picnics to various parks and waterways. We visited museums, art galleries, activity centres, aunts and uncles further afield from the local ones. We all had a great time and the children loved the time we spent together.

So, September arrived. The children went back to school, Tony started his new job, he didn't quite pass all of the exams — some of the Company Law was even too much for him, but he did become an Accountancy Technician, which is what the company wanted. Now he was only working around the corner, so he could come home for his lunch and as he finished at 5.00pm we saw each other for half an hour, as my new job with BT started at 6.00pm.

Again, I was in that state of being terrified and excited all at the same time, for I was finally going to do the job I had always wanted — to be a telephonist. The training was for ten weeks, after which time you were given a contract and had to sign the Official Secrets Act. Now not only was I going to be a telephonist but an international one at that! Can you imagine talking to people all over the world and GETTING PAID FOR IT? Wow!

I have to admit the training was really hard for me and there came a time around the seventh week when I thought of packing it in as I didn't seem to get a lot of it, but then it all suddenly fell into place and made perfect sense. It was a newly built telephone exchange and everyone was new. Some had transferred from London and other areas, and some like me were completely new to the job and the building. The duty rota was very varied but mainly it was three short evenings covering the hours of 6pm-10.30pm and two full nights of either 6pm-7am or 7pm-8am. There was lots of overtime and we were allowed to swap shifts with someone else, management were only interested in "bums on seats" and didn't mind who filled them.

It was a really exciting time for me, I loved the job with a passion and volunteered for overtime whenever there was any going. I made lots of new friends and as the building was right in the town centre there were plenty of places to go for a drink or a meal or just a get together after finishing the early shift. Not that I went very often, as I wanted to get back home to my family, but when I did go we had a real good laugh. Sometimes Tony would get a sitter in and come to join us, it was like the old party days.

About a couple of years after I started this job, I was asked to become a union rep. I had never been keen on unions but as this was a "Closed Shop" I thought I might as well give it a go. Sticking up for my fellow workers against the bosses was an eye-opener and of course it meant I had to attend a few meetings. I even called, "Everybody out," one night when the heating broke down and we were told to work with our coats on. It was really cold and below the legal guidelines the government set out, so I said, "No way, get some heaters in here then we will get back to work," and from somewhere they found quite a few fan heaters. SORTED.

So, we settled into a really comfortable time, which meant only one thing. Trouble was around the corner, and it came.

I had been working long hours by putting in lots of overtime. A friend said to me one night, "Carol, you should be careful how much overtime you do, if you do too much the taxman will take it back from you." Now, I have never been very good with maths and I had no idea how the taxman worked out our Pay As You Earn (PAYE). So, I didn't take much notice of what my friend had said, that is, until I got my next pay cheque. Then the penny dropped. It was true, my earnings were huge but so was the tax I had to pay on it all. It seemed I had been working half the week just for the taxman. This was a bitter blow for me but I learnt from that and always worked out (with ony's help) just how many hours I could work before the taxman could get his hands on it.

Tony had also been working a lot too, only I never realised how much he had been doing, until one day I was getting ready to go to work and Tony was laying on the settee. He looked really ill. I said, "Are you okay? You look a bit grey." He said it was just a bug and he would be fine, "Go to work and don't worry." Well, I did go to work but I did worry and one of my friends noticed. He asked me what was wrong, so I told him I was worried about Tony and how he looked. My friend told me to go home and call an ambulance because he thought Tony was having a heart attack. I laughed and said, "Don't be silly he's only 36." But my friend insisted, saying, "I was only 28 when something similar happened to me." So I did what he said. Good job I did, by the time I got back home, Tony was much worse. I called an ambulance. They only took a few minutes to get there and confirmed he was having a heart attack. They rushed him off to the hospital. My mum came and took the kids home with her, while I went to the hospital to find where they had taken Tony.

Two hours later after stabilising him, they let me into the Intensive Care Unit (ICU) where he was connected to lots of wires and machines. It was all very scary. The doctor told me he was off the critical list now but they wanted to keep an eye on him for a while longer. When he had been stable for a reasonable time they told us Tony's heart wall had hardened in places probably from all the poison that had been in his system for so long when his arm was playing up therefore making it more difficult to beat properly. He also had to cut down his working hours. I was a bit confused because as far as I knew he only worked 9am-5pm. It was then he told me he had been doing three other peoples' jobs, as when they had left, the management had not replaced them, just gave it all for Tony to do. Now the stress had shown what a bad idea that was.

I went to Tony's mum's shop, (they bought with his dad's retirement money) to give them something to do. I told her about his heart attack. She startled me by crying (being a person who never shown any feelings for anyone). It was a shock especially when she said with venom, "This is all your fault, if he didn't have to do so much for you and had not married you, my son would be perfectly all right now." Well, I didn't realise she felt that way about me and I went home feeling really miserable.

Tony had to have a long time off work while he recuperated. I found I was watching him all the time and wondering if it really was my fault. Tony was aware something was bothering me and eventually got out of me the conversation I'd had with his mother. He was not happy she had said such a thing, and assured me it was his own fault, for thinking he could do three jobs at once; furthermore, marrying me had been and was still the best thing he had ever done.

We really were blessed with two lovely children who were being very good; they helped so much, by being quiet and getting Daddy a drink or a book so he didn't have to get too tired.

As he improved he said he had seen a bigger house and thought we should buy it. He was right, it was twice as big as our little terrace. I fell in love with it straight away so off we go again. I was worried still about Tony's heart but he said he felt fine and would soon be back at work so we might as well move before he was, I didn't take much persuading. The house was still a terrace but it had a reception room, a lounge, a dining room, kitchen, three massive bedrooms, and a bathroom. The stairs swirled around in a dog-leg style, and all the windows were huge. We moved in straight away, it didn't need anything doing to it and our house sold within a week to a cash buyer.

I felt we were now living in a palace and Tony was getting stronger so life was good. The doctor still wanted Tony to stay home a while longer, he had to go to many different clinics and yoga classes before he was finally discharged.

When he did finally go back to work, there was some new staff and so the pressure was off, but, after a few weeks back at work Tony was told they were letting him go, as they didn't want to have staff who might keel over with a heart attack while at work. In other words, he was a health risk. They were not prepared to have him on pay. They gave him three months' pay and said he should go straight away. Because of his knowledge of their accounts, they didn't want him to work his notice, in case he sabotaged things, as if he would. Tony has never been a vindictive or revengeful man. But they didn't know him like I did. I think they just waited until he had been back long enough for them to release him without any repercussion coming back at them.

Now for another decision. I was worried about Tony finding a new job with all the stress that brings yet, so we talked about it and decided, it would be good if he stayed home, looked after the children and the house, while I went to work, as my wages were very good and we could easily manage. Also, we thought of the children, I still would not let them play outside on the roads, they were too busy. Thinking about my childhood I realised it wasn't fair for them, they need fresh air. So we sold our beautiful big home, moved out of town and bought a bungalow for the grand total of £16,500 in a small town called Shepshed.

It was so easy in those days to buy and sell a property. The children could now go outside and play, something we never allowed them to do in the town. They loved it and made many friends. Of course this also changed for us too, as our children went around to their friends' homes, sometimes their friends would come into ours, so instead of two children at the table sometimes there were four or five. Instant families! It was all SO worth it — our children blossomed with all this country air and freedom. I also relaxed more as they still seemed so strong and no sign of my disability in either of them. Apart from the usual child illnesses they seemed to be very healthy.

New Technology

When we moved, we also decided to try some new technology for our new home. We bought a microwave oven as our ordinary cooker had done too many moves and wasn't working properly. This microwave was state of the art and it was BIG. There was a list of menus on a flip control at the side of the door above the switches and settings. According to all the adverts it was a faster, safer, easier, cheaper way to cook.

But it was a totally new way to cook and one should remember that when cooking the food. Of course, I knew this but when it came to timings I really did not believe that a potato in the jacket could cook in 5-8 minutes (they take about an hour in a standard cooker).

Of course, there is NO WAY a sponge cake will cook in three minutes, so disbeliever me cooked a cake for eight minutes. We watched it rise beautifully to three minutes then we watched it start to shrink until the eight minutes was up and when it came out the oven it was solid as a brick. There was no breaking it.

We threw it outside and some poor bird tried to break it but I am sure it damaged its beak instead. So yes, I did learn the hard way. Once we had gotten the hang of this way to cook, it really was easier, cleaner, tastier and cheaper (our electricity bills went down).

We cooked most of our meals using it. There were actually some things it would not cook like Yorkshire pudding, pastry and roast potatoes, so for them we used our Baby Belling.

When I told friends at work about it they came up with some dire warnings, "Don't watch it, you will go blind." "Don't stand near it, you'll get radiation." "Don't eat anything hot, you'll be scalded."

Actually, that was true if you tried to eat something straight from the cooker, as the microwaves are still moving for at least a minute after the bell has gone off, therefore you have to take another minute off some cooking times and let the food rest.

Memories Of Children's TV.

How Many Do You Remember?

Fury
This is the range country where the pounding hooves of untamed horses still thunder in mountains, meadows and canyons. Every herd has its own leader, but there is only one Fury — Fury, King of the Wild Stallions. And here in the wild west of today, hard-riding men still battle the open range for a living — men like Jim Newton, owner of the Broken Wheel Ranch and Pete, his top hand, who says he cut his teeth on a branding iron.

Black Beauty
Black Beauty is a pure black, thoroughbred horse in late 19th Century rural England who is adopted into the household of James Gordon, a local doctor and widower, and befriended by his daughter, son Kevin, and their friends. Each week the children get involved in an adventure that brings them into contact with all sorts of colourful characters and villains. You can always be assured, however, that Beauty is on hand to help save the day.

Champion the Wonder Horse
The series starred Barry Curtis as 12-year-old Ricky North, who lived on his uncle's ranch in the American Southwest. Ricky's uncle, Sandy North, was played by Jim Bannon. Ricky's companions were a wild stallion, Champion, and a German Shepherd dog, Rebel, played by Blaze.

Lassie
I grew up with the "Lassie" series. I just loved that dog and thought it would be great to have one just like it. Looking back on it, I would say that I was addicted to that show. Lassie lived on the Miller farm with Jeff the boy and Mum and Gramps. They had many exciting adventures.

The Littlest Hobo
London is an extremely intelligent, wandering German Shepherd who walks into a different place in each episode of this long-running television series, and comes upon people down on their luck or in trouble. London always befriends and helps the struggling person or persons. Then, when his job is done at episode's end, London declines to be the pet of the people he has helped and departs to continue his cross-country drifting.

Follyfoot
Young Dora is sent to stay with her uncle on his farm in rural England while her parents travel overseas for a year. Seeing as she has a love for horses, her uncle suggests she visit Follyfoot Farm, which is a part of his estate that looks after unwanted and unloved horses. It is only here that Dora feels truly happy, but what will happen when her parents return?

Skippy
I thought as a kid that this show was really nice. The theme song is wonderful, and stuck in my head for a long while, and the Australian locations are really striking. But Skippy the Kangaroo steals the show, he is really cute and endearing not to mention smart. Overall, a nice show that was worth watching for Skippy and the scenery.

Bill and Ben

I loved this show for the very young. It was a make-believe — two flowerpot men that came to life when the gardener wasn't about, getting into all sorts of mischief. They did speak strange but children seemed to understand them. They lived in two big flowerpots and standing in between them was the Little Weed who would shout 'WEEEEED' to warn Bill and Ben the gardener was coming back. They would jump into their big pots and the gardener never knew they were there.

Rag, Tag and Bobtail

There were three main characters: Rag, a hedgehog; Tag, a mouse; and Bobtail, a rabbit; five baby rabbits also appeared occasionally. All the characters were glove puppets, operated by Sam and Elizabeth Williams. The stories were simple and there were no catch-phrases as there were in other programs in the cycle, but the series is still remembered with affection.

Muffin the Mule

Is a puppet character in British television for children. The original programs featuring the character were presented by Annette Mills, sister of John Mills and broadcast live by the BBC from their studios from 1946 to 1952. Mills and the puppet continued with programs that were broadcast until 1955, when Mills died. The shows were then shown on ITV in 1956 and 1957. A modern animated version of Muffin appeared on the BBC in 2005.

The Woodentops

Was a children's television series first shown on BBC in 1955 and featured on the Friday edition of Watch with Mother. The main characters were a family of wooden dolls who lived on a farm Daddy, Mummy, Jenny, Willy, and Baby Woodentop. The children, Jenny and Willy, were twins. Other characters included: Buttercup the Cow, Spotty Dog (or, as announced at the start of each episode, "The very biggest spotty dog you ever did see"), Mrs Scrubbitt (who comes to "help" Mrs Woodentop), and Sam Scrubbitt (who helps Daddy Woodentop with the animals). Curiously, Daddy Woodentop never wore a shirt and spoke with a country yokel accent, whilst Mummy and the twins were both extremely well-dressed and well-spoken. Mrs Scrubbitt was suitably reserved.

Of course, there were many more, like Medic, Dragnet, Zorro, The Lone Ranger, Rawhide, Wagon Train, Dr Who, etc., but these are the ones I particularly liked and remember with affection.

Country Living

Living out in the country was much better for all. I had to leave for work a few minutes earlier than when we were in the town but it was a lovely drive and I enjoyed driving just as much now as I first had. Of course, it was more difficult in the winter as the snow used to lay deeply. Sometimes going home at 6.00am some of the roads seemed to have disappeared, there were no other tyre tracks to follow so I had to drive very slowly. I gauged it by using the hedgerows on either side and as I was the only one on the road I went right down the middle. I really don't know what I would have done had anything gone wrong, as we didn't have mobile phones and there were no phone boxes on that stretch of road. I guess I would have had to sit and wait for someone to come along, but thank goodness, I never had to.

After a couple of years, Tony felt good and got a job in the next town — two miles away. It was in the opposite direction to the city where I worked and for a while, I had to take him to work and fetch him home. He was on 9am-5pm and I was 6pm-8am so the only time we saw each other on my duty days was in the car going back and forth to his work, but that was only for a few weeks as he got a small motorbike so he could be more independent.

There was a scare in the control centre where I worked. BT had been recruiting lots more staff, quite a few were foreigners and one of them took ill with tuberculosis (TB) so we all had to go and have an x-ray. My doctor called me to his office and told me the x-ray showed no TB but it did show I had scoliosis and my spine was curving to the left. He said it was only a slight curve and nothing to worry about, so I didn't.

Sometimes things didn't go to plan of course, a couple of things come to mind that make us smile now but not then. Once, I shut the front door, but had left my keys inside. All the windows were closed. So I said to Jason, "Here you go son, break that window, you have my permission." Every boy's dream, I think. Unfortunately, he picked up a house brick and literally threw it with all his might. He broke the window for sure into a thousand bits. Ha-ha, good job it was only single-glazed. (Never had double-glazing in those days.) He then carefully climbed in and got the keys so we could go and fetch dad.

That was an expensive lesson — to make sure you always have your keys before closing the door. The window was in Jason's bedroom and there were shards of glass everywhere, so all the bedding had to go, along with the carpet. There was no way we were going to get it all out so it had to go. The rest took ages to get rid of.

Another time I rushed out of the house forgetting I had put some eggs on to boil for tea — oops. When we got back home, the place was full of smoke, the alarms going full pelt and the smell was horrendous. Fortunately, the only damage was to the pan, it had melted and the eggs had exploded all over the ceiling. Yuk!

Tony and the kids built a lovely big pond in the garden. We had fun going to get some fish and plants, pump/fountain. We didn't have a clue as to what was best or how to look after them, but the people serving gave us some useful information — silly me thought all you had to do was put them in the pond and feed them once a day. I didn't realise how many illnesses fish could get, so we had to have a quarantine tank too, not that it did much good, the fish still died. Those that stayed healthy did look good and it was very calming sitting by the pond watching them. You have to feed them at the same time every day and after a while the fish knew it was feeding time and would come to the edge and wait for the food. They would even take it from your hand.

One hot summer day, Colette was tormenting our little dog and saying it needed to cool down, so, she dropped it into the pond and made it swim back to her. Tony did no more than pick up Colette and dropped her into the pond too! Ooh - yuk! She thought it was hilarious; I don't think the fish were impressed though.

Tony and I went for our first holiday abroad. My parents came and stayed with the children (which would please Jason immensely as his granddad let him drink his whiskey) while we flew off into the sun.

It was the most terrifying time of my life when that plane took off. I was holding Tony's hand so tight I nearly cut off his circulation... but the elation once we were up was fabulous. Looking at the fields and buildings getting smaller was strange and that little voice said again, "It's not natural for humans to fly," which had me worried when we came into land in Majorca. The town we were staying in was called "Callor Millor" a 40-minute drive away from the airport. That was another thing; they all drove on the wrong side of the road. Eeeeeeek!

There were so many new sounds and smells to take in, good job we were here for two weeks. The sunshine was so beautiful. Someone told me it was a different kind of heat abroad, I didn't know what they meant until we got there. It's hard to describe but it was gentle, apart from the hours of 12-4pm, that's when the wise ones took a siesta in the shade. There was a continual warm breeze too which helped the cooling process. During the time I was there, we noticed I didn't limp or feel any pain, all movement was so much easier. If only it could be like this at home. Also looking around there didn't seem to be ANY disabled local people, even the really old looking ones still seemed to have a spring in their step.

Our hotel was right on the sea front. There were three cooked meals a day which were all very tasty, although, I did find it strange not being able to drink the water from the tap. We had to have bottled water always, but the beer was good. I was lucky I never got any tummy trouble but poor Tony did, he was really ill for a couple of days. The chemist gave us some medication but it didn't work. Tony resorted to drastic measures and ate a whole garlic raw, he said it tasted foul and his breath smelt of it but it worked. His tummy stopped hurting, and for the rest of the holiday all was well. Another thing we saw was a policeman on every street corner carrying a machine gun. There was no unruly drunken violence in this town! We all partied through the early hours having lots of fun. The two weeks went quickly, we had had a fabulous time, but we were both looking forward to getting back home to the children. We had bought them lots of presents and agreed next time we went they were going too.

Life seemed idyllic so what went wrong this time? Well, I guess it was me, since we had moved to the country. Tony was no longer able to get to join us for a meal or a drink after work, nor did he want to speak much. He spent most of his free time reading, and although I loved my family I needed something else. Only trouble was I didn't know what. All I knew was it felt like something was missing from my life. Which sounds silly when I had more than most people ever get.

Part of it came from my new friend (who I had been warned from others not to have anything to do with her as she was trouble) — again, the Demon in me says, "They say don't, so you know you must." Well, I like to believe there is good in all people and I had tried to prove the doubters wrong I guess. Only this time it didn't work. She would talk when she was supposed to work and thought nothing of chatting to the customers; she even put some of the calls through to me. I thought it seemed like fun and I broke one of the cardinal rules at work and started to fraternise with the customers. Sometimes we would arrange to meet them after work, and she would say things to me like, "What a shame you're married, we could have so much fun if you were free."

This went on for many weeks until my supervisor took me to one side and told me to "Stop ruining your life by doing what you know is wrong." It was a bit of a shock, but it did make me realise I was being very stupid and risking everything for a person who really was bad. After re-evaluating my situation, I told her I wouldn't be seeing her any more. She sneered at me, told me I was like all the rest, and walked off. We never spoke again.

I took a few days off and told Tony how stupid I had been. Well, of course, he knew something had been going on but was too much of a gentleman to say. I told him I was confused as to where I wanted to be. Tony said I needed some space to sort myself out. We agreed being apart for a while might be a good idea. I went and stayed at my parents' house for a few days (as they were away for a few weeks). I could be totally alone for a time. I didn't know what I wanted; divorce had even been mentioned. Tony said he didn't want that, but he did want me to be happy, that was his only goal in life.

I had never been completely on my own before and I was realising I didn't like it. I went shopping, supposedly for food and came back with vodka, but drowning your sorrows definitely does not help. I started thinking again, did I really want to carry on with this shallow life and give up the best thing that's ever happened to me, or did I want to resume my family life? WHAT WAS WRONG WITH ME? Am I stupid or what? I felt like I had hit a brick wall, crushed and broken. I just sat and stared into nothing feeling totally lost and alone.

Then, during this soul-searching time, something **REALLY** strange happened. When I was at rock bottom and thought there was nothing I could do to make it right - **I FELT**

THIS WARMTH ENVELOP ME as if someone were putting their arms around me giving me a hug and a voice said, **"GO TO TONY."** I looked around but there really was no one there but me. Spooky.

Even though it was very late at night, I did go to Tony and told him what had happened. He gave me a strange look and said, "The same thing has just happened to me too." I said, "Well what does it mean?" Tony said, "It was a message from God telling us everything will be all right. If we want to try again we should start to build bridges."

Now I have never been a religious person. When I was young our parents made us go to church and Sunday school (my brothers said that was to give them a couple of hours' peace). I have never felt comfortable in a church, I felt more like an intruder. Now here was Tony telling me we had had a message from God. We sat down, talked all through the night, and decided we should move nearer to parents… again!

Tony's mum and dad were told we were having a few problems. They agreed we should move over to their village. There were a few houses for sale and we had a choice. The one we chose was a semi with the longest garden I had ever seen and it backed onto allotments, so no one overlooked us.

The only problem was it needed some TLC and when the builders and electricians came they told us we had to be out of the place while they fixed it up. We went and stayed with Tony's mum and dad AGAIN. At least they only lived a few doors down so we could keep an eye on progress with our house.

When it was finally done, we moved back in. I decided we needed a new bed so one day Colette and I went off into town bed hunting.

In one shop that we went into we were approached by a very good-looking young salesman. I was feeling mischievous while trying the beds and asked him to join me so I could see how it would feel with two of us on it (after all, Tony would be sharing it with me). Well, you should have seen the look on Colette's face. She said, "MOTHER, BEHAVE," and the poor young man went very red. Ha-ha-ha-ha.

Tony got a job with the city council with the Cremations and Burials Office and I transferred to days. The children were enrolled into their new schools and made new friends. (They were good at that because of all the moves they had made.)

We went to the local Methodist church and found it interesting. The people seemed friendly, and they did all love to sing, as did I, so much so I joined the choir. Tony had a chat with the Minister and said he would like to become a minister (a minister in the Methodist church is the same as a vicar in the Church of England or a priest in the Catholic Church). Well, the answer was, "You can try, it's very hard work and there are lots of exams to take, but if you're serious I can put you forward," and so he did.

The work really was hard, (who would have thought ministers worked more than one day a week? In reality, it's more like 24/7) but Tony put his all into it. First, he had to become a local preacher, and then he went on to college for the ministry, that would be a three-year slog.

Now our very long garden came in handy. As Tony worked on it he said he got his best sermon ideas while he worked the soil. (Most of them really were good.) He wasn't a hellfire and damnation preacher but his messages were powerful and made you really think about life and its consequences. Colette thought it would be a hoot to join the Girls' Brigade, as they often went off for weekends away. She certainly did not join for the religion.

We all became involved so much into the church life, I was a Sunday school teacher, Jason joined the Boys' Brigade, and I eventually joined the Girls' Brigade too as an officer. More exams for us all.

Tony and I also got involved with fund raising and would often man a stall selling cakes, bric-a-brac, clothes, books, etc.

We did car boot sales. I even booked Mallory Park Race track for the kids, to do a sponsored bike ride, now that was a fun day. Also, there were the day trips to arrange so we could all go off and have a fun time. Somehow, I even ended up being the editor of the church magazine, which came out once a month.

The Jury

I experienced another situation: Tony did warn me not to do it as I could have gotten out of it because of my disability, but I thought it would be good and I would be doing something useful. What was it? JURY SERVICE. I was called to go to the Crown Court where I may be picked for a jury; well in fact I was. It was for a sexual abuse case.

We had to sit in the court and listen to hours of legal talk, most of which I am sure none of us understood. The case was against a headmaster who apparently abused children in his care, by sitting them on his knees and cuddling them when they were upset or hurt or even just learning to read from the book the teacher was holding.

Now I am and always have been a very broadminded person and as I was listening to all this, I thought, "What a lot of rubbish, we do that in Sunday school, Girls' Brigade, Shell group, etc., ('Shell group' was for children aged three to five years old, meeting once a week for games, crafts and other activities). I know my own children have been comforted that way at school when they were upset." Not once did I ever think of it as sexual abuse, but according to the Law: *IF YOU TOUCH ANOTHER PERSON EVEN ON THE SHOULDER WITHOUT THEIR PERMISSION, IT IS CLASSED AS SEXUAL ABUSE.*

So, for ten days we had to sit and listen to children being brought in as witnesses to this abuse. Some were as young as six years old; all were terrified of the court and the officers and were very often in floods of tears. No one was allowed to touch them and console them. It all seemed very cold and calculating.

When the jury finally had to retire for the verdict, it seemed I was the only one who thought it was all over the top and a waste of time. One juror asked me how I would feel if my child had been subject to "that sort of thing." When I said they had, and it was fine, they said I was a bad parent and should be up there with the headmaster. So, the verdict was not unanimous but 11-1 guilty. Therefore, the headmaster was sent down for five years and would go on the Paedophile Register. Vandals and bigots chased his wife and four children out of their home, they lost everything.

I went home devastated and really worried as to what this would mean now in all the groups at church where children were involved. Obviously, I never touched anyone for a long time after that. We were paid very well for the privilege of being on the jury but I have to say I will NEVER DO IT AGAIN. It just is not worth all the hurt and conflict that follows. Whoever it was that said, "the law is an ass" must have been on one of these juries too. It seems the barristers were only happy when they scored against each other, with no feelings for the hurt they were bringing to everyone else.

All this and a full-time job, plus helping to look after our home. Something had to give, unfortunately for me it was my job. I had never settled down since transferring to days (I am more of a night person, always was). I was having a lot of sick days (we are only allowed 17 per year and I exceeded that). I also started to lose my patience with the customers and argued with them. Well, we all know the customer is ALWAYS RIGHT... but I didn't agree and told them so. The supervisors noted all this and reports went in. I was called into the manager's office and was told to "pull my socks up or be dismissed." After another few days off sick the personnel officer came to our home and told me they wanted to terminate my contract. I had two choices:

1) I could carry on taking time off until I was dismissed and claim one year's unemployment benefit and not necessarily get another job, or:

2) I could take medical retirement with a lump sum and a lifetime pension.

I took the pension.

And so, the beginning of 1985 it all took just a few short weeks to finalise everything, the end of the best job I had ever had. But I was moving on and putting all my energy into the church, trying to help as many people as I could. I visited people who couldn't get out, did shopping for them, and took them to their doctor's appointments.

Life sure was busy and I started to feel tired and suffering more pain. My doctor told me to take paracetamol at regular times, and as long as I only took the recommended dosage there was no danger in taking them long term. He said it was better to keep the pain down than wait for it to get bad. "Prevention was better than cure" according to him. He too found it fascinating that no one knew what my condition was ' …a kind of Muscular Dystrophy' was still the nearest anyone came up with. He also suggested I get a walking stick; I laughed and said I wasn't old enough yet. He replied, "You don't have to be old to need help, if your muscles are weak and you lose your balance, using a stick will help." OK, that made sense, so I got one. I did feel very conscious of it at first, but the doc was right it did help, and it didn't take long for me to stop being conscious of it. It was certainly a big help walking up and down the hill to church, which I seemed to be spending more time at.

One of our congregation called Tom, took a real shine to Tony and me, he seemed to be there where ever we went. Talking to him we discovered he was a very lonely man who apparently had no friends or family. His wife had divorced him many years ago, leaving him alone in his house. We sometimes invited him into our home for a meal or just to chat. This went on for many months. Then he was told he had cancer. He was very upset, as anyone would be. It fell upon Tony or me to take Tom to the hospital for his chemotherapy, etc. He eventually seemed to get over that, as they told him he was in remission. So he resumed his Sunday school teachings, feeling blessed to be able to do so as he never had children of his own.

About this time, I had to go down to Torquay and help my mum as my dad was dying and she needed some respite. Because I was no longer working it fell on me. I was down there for three weeks. Mum refused the vicar permission to talk to Dad before he passed on (she was still in denial) and a few days later we were having to arrange the funeral. Thank goodness my youngest brother sorted that out. He also helped keep Mum calm more than I could. I was told I had to go see my dad now he was at rest and furthermore I had to touch him to say goodbye otherwise I would forget him. Well, I have to say I did see and touch him BUT that was not my dad lying there and I regretted being there. I was never going to forget him anyway, now all I remember is the cold emptiness.

Tom, had become so attached to Tony and me he told everyone we were his adopted brother and sister and indeed he was at our home more than his own. This was having a bad effect on our daughter. She had gotten to the rebellious stage and in a few weeks, she would be sixteen. Oh, joy!

One day she told us she was going into town for a job interview. She gave us all the details and we thought no more of it, until hours later, we still had not heard from her and she had not come back to the village. None of her friends knew where she was. We rang the place she was going for the interview and they told us she never showed. This was at a time when two sixteen-year-old girls called Lynda Mann and Dawn Ashcroft, had been brutally killed just a mile down the road, so you can imagine how distraught we were feeling. The police told us to call back tomorrow as no one is classed as missing until twenty-four hours have passed. OMG!

Obviously neither of us had any sleep that night hoping we would hear her come in. She didn't. The police finally came around and asked lots of questions, took a photo of her to be distributed and told us to go through her room and if she had a diary to look through that too, it might give a clue as to where she was. Well, it didn't do that, but it certainly did let us know how resentful she was of Tom taking her parents away from her. We hadn't had a clue she felt that way, she always seemed so happy when we were all together. Now we had to stay home and wait for a call, so you can imagine how strung out we were every time the phone rang, and it was another caring person asking if we had heard anything yet?

That went on for ten days and nights — we were a pair of wrecks when the police knocked on the door holding onto a dirty girl with a scowl on her face. They all came in and the first thing Colette said was, "If you think I am staying here after I am sixteen you're wrong and the law says you can't make me." I said, "Is that right?" to the officer and he replied, "Yes, they can legally leave home when they turn sixteen." That gave us three days to try and find out what was wrong and how we could put it right. She also looked very strange as she had become a GOTH and only wore black clothes and black make-up apart from the face having very white skin. Ugh. I was told it was just a phase and she would grow out of it - Lord, I hoped so. She went around the village wearing a flowing black robe and scaring the kids. She thought it was hilarious.

We knew she resented our time with Tom but we couldn't turn our backs on him, as his cancer had come back and he needed help. But so too did Colette, so we had to find the right balance, if that was possible. Of course it wasn't; being so rebellious and determined, Colette was out to show how tough she was and no matter what anyone did or said, it wasn't right. So, we gave her a birthday party. All her friends came and tried to get her to stay, but she was determined to leave home the next day. We asked her where she was going and she said she was going back to the squat where her real friends were. We said, "OK if that's what you want, just please keep in touch and if you ever want to come home your room will be here." What more could we do? It was better for her to go knowing she could come back anytime, than to go off and never hear from her. It was a really difficult time for us; Jason came and hugged me saying he would never do this to us. I think he meant that at the time.

We tried to get back into some sort of routine; at least we knew where Colette was. Tony still had studying to do, plus all the other things to do with the church. I did resign from the Girl's Brigade to give me a little more time at home, though I was still fundraising, editing the magazine, and Sunday school. Tom still came for his evening meal with us — it had become a regular thing now, and I was surprised at the attitude of certain people in the church who were saying that we were spoiling Tom and should send him packing, because he was taking advantage of our kindness. I could not believe I was hearing this from so-called Christians. He was a lonely, frightened man, who now had a death penalty over him, as the cancer had come back with a vengeance. He was only 53 and had months to live at the most, we couldn't just drop him. Looking at the clothes he wore, he didn't have any money either. We were a little concerned as he had told us he had no relatives, we were the nearest he had. We had also been to his home a few times to help him clean up, but to be honest we couldn't do much as he was a hoarder. There were piles of papers EVERYWHERE. He owned a three-bedroomed detached and every room was piled high. Apparently, he couldn't bear to throw anything away and he had dated every paper too, including all junk mail. Someone was going to have fun clearing this out when he passed on.

Well, we found out who when he was admitted into the 'LOROS' Hospice — for the last few weeks of his life. He told us he had left everything to us in his homemade will. That was too much. Tony and I discussed it and we talked with Tom the next day saying we were not too happy and asked if Tom had a solicitor. He did and we called them and arranged for someone to come and help Tom sort out his estate. Thank goodness we did, as Tom in a more lucid moment realised, he did have some friends whom he would like to help, even if he hadn't heard from them in a long while.

It turned out he did have a lot of money and it was shared out eight ways including a good sum to the church, but he still left his house and all within it to Tony and me. We had the job of clearing it out — which wasn't as easy as we first thought because Tom had hidden money in between the sheets of paper that were stacked up all through the house. We found hundreds of pounds and asked the solicitor what we should do with it, they told us if it was in the house then it was now legally ours and we could do whatever we wanted with it. It took quite a few weeks and six big skips to clear all the papers out. The solicitors were great, they dealt with all the finances and the funeral — a few surprises popped up there too, suddenly he had relatives from all over the place. All wondering if they would get a share in his money. Where were they when he really needed them? The only people who visited Tom in the hospice regularly were, Tony, Jason, Colette, me and our church minister.

Yes, Colette had finally seen the light and came home. It was such a relief with all this other stuff going on. She got a job in the village post office too so she was near home all the time and it **seemed** the Goth look was out. Phew! She still liked to shock though and did put the black on sometimes. I could live with that, she was home and safe.

We also got a nasty shock from certain members of the church, when they found out Tom had left his house to us, they said we only befriended him for his money. Oh, how people do turn, funny really, a few months before they were telling us, Tom was taking advantage. Geeeeeez.

When Tom finally passed on and all his estate was finalised, we decided to take a holiday. As promised we all went to one of the Canary Isles called Fuerteventura. It was the least populated of the islands, and it was very flat, so much so they had to import all the water in tankers, where it was stored underground in massive tanks. There was nothing but sea, sand and sun — we chose it for that reason. We all just needed to chill out for a while. The plane still freaked me out, but the rest was fabulous. We all had a great time. Two wonderful weeks in fairy land, then it was back to reality.

Well, we did try to get back to normal, but living in a closed village is never easy and we were still classed as outsiders. There was a lot of resentment from many that we had Tom's house, which I didn't know what to do with. We couldn't keep going over to keep an eye on it and the house market was in the doldrums, nothing was selling anywhere.

Colette came up with a temporary solution; she wanted to live in it with a couple of her friends. Well, now, if there's any way to rile up narrow-minded villagers, that's the way to do it! Woo-hoo -- we did it good. Funnily enough no one ever said a bad word to Colette I think they were worried to approach her, as she could still dress in the GOTHIC clothes and often walked around the village all in black with her white painted face, when she wanted to cause a stir. She did look formidable.

Tony was told that as a minister of the cloth his children should behave better, which was a bit premature of them as Tony was still training and had not taken his final exams yet. He really was not "a man of the cloth" but Jason who was still a quiet unassuming boy was picked on a lot and the final straw was when our neighbour threatened to break Jason's legs if he ever even so much as looked at their dog again. (When they were talking to us before he used to fuss it and take it walks for them which they were very pleased about.)

Well, that was it, I had had enough, so we put the house on the market. We knew it would take a long time to sell but my brother was selling his house in Leicester and was desperate to move his family down to Plymouth where he was working, so we moved into their house with a bridging loan until ours was sold.

In the meantime, Colette, rebel that she was, invited her latest boyfriend to go and live with her. Can you imagine the stir that caused with the villagers? Wow, she knew how to stir 'em up, but she revelled in it. She was still working in the village post office and never once did anyone say a thing to her. No, they complained to our minister telling him we should have more control over our family, but the law says she is old enough to look after herself and she did. She did tell us that her and Pete wanted to get married, so we started making plans though Tony and I were dubious because she was only just coming up to 17 years old. We thought it was a bit young but knew not to argue with her. Colette and I went shopping; we found the most gorgeous wedding dress and were having silk bouquets made. At the trial dressing Colette looked like a beautiful princess — stunning really. Shame we were the only ones to see her because however there was a twist, as there usually is somewhere in the Williams' world.

One day I went to the house to talk about the reception, she was limping and having trouble breathing. I asked what was the matter, she said, "Nothing really. I fell down the stairs." Another friend who was also living in the house took me to one side and said that Colette did not fall down the stairs, Pete had kicked her down them and then continued kicking her around the house, all because she told him to get his own tea.

When I confronted Colette, she told me that was the truth. Without further ado, I told her to pack a bag, she was coming home with me whether she liked it or not. Surprisingly she did as she was told — now there's a first! The next thing I did was tell Pete to pack his bags and get out. Colette finally told me Pete had been beating her up for weeks, because she wouldn't wait on him hand and foot (he was a Geordie boy — and apparently it was allowed in his home and indeed expected that the woman does man's bidding). Yeah right, not in our family it's not.

That's what someone told me who lives in the North of England, and that's what they expect from their women at that time (hopefully things have changed today). He seemed such a charming boy. Just goes to show how wrong you can be about a person.

Tony and I both agreed this wedding was going no further until we got things sorted. Colette seemed relieved, but she was also terrified that Pete would come and get her, so she went and stayed with another friend and his mum, knowing they would protect her because Pete was scared of him.

Pete's father came to our house and asked us why we had cancelled the wedding. We told him our daughter was not marrying anyone who beat and kicked her about. I could not believe I was hearing right when he said, "Well if she won't do as she's told, what do you expect? She has got to know her place!" We told him our daughter was never going to be anyone's punch-bag and lackey, so he had better go and hopefully we will never see either of you again.

I can see why Colette was frightened enough not to stay at our home, as Pete came around lots of times demanding to see her and telling us we had no right to stop him seeing her and we had to let her marry him. Where do these people come from? Then he changed tack and started crying and begging us to let him see her so she would go back to him because he loved her so much. Yeah, right. No chance.

I also could also see why Colette thought she would be safe with her friend. He was one scary looking boy, sporting a Mohican haircut and tattoos and some body-piercings. He really did look fierce but Colette said he was a quiet gentle person, unless you crossed him. Oooh-eeerr.

So here we are, moving day. The date is 06/07/89, bet there's not many dates like that in the calendar. My brother had been desperate to get his family back together again as he had been living down in Plymouth where he was now working and at last that came to be, so we had helped each other really. I could not have lived in that village much longer with all those two-faced hypocrites, they were so unbelievable, and nothing like the Christians they profess to be.

Moving in went quite smoothly, (we were getting good at it by now) the longest wait we had was for BT to come and fix us up with a telephone line. How my brother's family had managed without one I do not know.

I have always liked this house as I used to come here every week visiting. Our children would all go off to play together, while Linda and I had a good chat. Sometimes Paul would be there too when he wasn't working. Although my visits did stop when I found out she had been having an affair with my older brother, having an affair is bad enough but with your brother-in-law is just too low. (She always thought they would go off to

Paradise together. He said it was offered so he took it!) No wonder Paul wanted to move his family away.

Now as it was July, we had to get sorted, because it was also a very busy time for us in the church. We had joined the main church in town now. I was part of the office staff with lots to do, as it was the yearly Methodist Conference time, which takes place in a different city every year, and this time it was our turn in Leicester. So we were in charge of all the organising. Can you imagine what was involved? Hundreds of clergy and their spouses from all over the country and even a few from overseas, were meeting here and we had to make the arrangements for their accommodation, meals, travel expenses, photos, identity badges, lectures, etc. It was very hectic, hard work but fun. I found it was one of the things I was really good at — organising. I was in my element. It had taken us many months to get all this put together, but, even with all the careful planning, things still went wrong of course, but on the day, we sorted out most problems, eventually.

Oh, how I loved those days. I felt so useful, apart from having to learn how to work on the computer the office had bought (to make our lives easier - HAH)! It was all done in DOS, no Windows around in those days! Things went pretty smoothly.

While I was doing that, Tony was in Wales at the college in Aberystwyth, taking his final exams for the Ministry. He would be away for a few days. Jason came with me to the conference and helped out as he was on his last year's school holiday. He too seemed to be enjoying himself and was extremely helpful doing my running around for me (he still wanted to protect me from doing too much). Now he was fifteen he was starting to fill out a little and was growing taller. He had a short time left before going out to work. I wanted him to go to a music college as he, like his sister, had a gift for art. Jason's, for music: He could play the piano, the organ and the guitar. Even though he said he couldn't read a note he could play anything you asked; but just like his sister he said he wasn't good enough to go to college. When he was younger he used to love the classics but just lately he started playing heavy metal and was in to 'Metallica.' He got quite upset when he heard me playing 'Stairway to Heaven' by Rolf Harris; he reckoned Rolf had ruined a real great piece of music.

He really had his heart set on joining the army. That depended on his final exam results and of course he had to pass the physicals to get in. He passed everything but the eye test. That was a bitter blow for him but in true Williams' style he picked himself up and looked for something else.

At home we were settling down nicely, but were very reluctant to mix with anyone around us. Although the neighbours seemed friendly we tended to keep to ourselves. We didn't ignore them or be rude, we would say hello when they were in the garden but that's as far as it went. After all that happened in that village, I am not sure I ever wanted to mix with people again, which would be very awkward if Tony did become a full-time minister as the wife is expected to help with certain duties. But I am more of a people person so I thought I would sort it out as I went along. I was really looking forward to it in many ways and of course the life of a minister is very varied and they are only allowed to be in one parish for a maximum of seven years. Then they have to move to a new area — with our track record for moving it suited us perfectly.

The council had decided to split Tony's job instead of him working full time. They now wanted him to "job share" so his hours were cut down. He now only worked 9-1, which we both thought was great. That gave us more time to be together and he had more time to give to the parishioners, which he could do even more. So now he had a driving licence again, that was another adjustment he had to make. Although he could drive big vehicles in the army he had let his licence expire when he left the service because he hated driving. I had been driving him around and waited outside while he went in to help whoever had called him. Now he had his own car so when he got a call out at a late hour, I could stay in home, warm and snug.

When I got my first driving licence, it was like a little red book with pages for your driving records (we had to renew our driving licence every three years up to 1973). Then they changed it to a paper licence which you had to renew every ten years. Then in the late 1990s they brought in the picture licence so you had the paper and a plastic card with your photo which is for life or if you become too ill to drive anymore. Now, the only time you have to let the Driver and Vehicle Licensing Agency (DVLA) have your licence back is if you move house (it's a £1,000 fine if you don't tell them).

Colette was still staying at her friend's house with his mum and it seemed she felt safer with him, even though Pete had finally got the message and didn't come around anymore. So, all in all life was good.

When Tony eventually got the results from his exams, we were very disappointed. He did pass, and actually got an A+ for his final dissertation, but could not be ordained because he was too much of an "enigma." According to the dictionary, *"A person that is mysterious, puzzling or difficult to understand - A riddle or paradox."*

Funny, he's been working for free all these years now, they refuse him a full ministry because he's an enigma. After all his hard work, it seems such a stupid thing, brings out the cynic in me because they know he will carry on doing what he loves for free, and he can do everything a minister can except give communion.

Apparently, the Methodist Church is THE hardest to enter as an ordained minister, more so than even the Catholic Church. That was a big blow to us but it didn't put Tony off, he was offered a position with the URC (United Reform Church) which he did on a part time basis because he still wanted to be part of the Methodist church. Now he was spending his time between the two. Fortunately, they were both in the same area.

Jason was now working in an engineering factory making tools. It was 15 miles away, across the other side of town and he got on his pushbike every day to get there and come home. He loved that job and was working hard, so on his 16th birthday we bought him a small motor bike to make his journey to and fro easier — though I have to say it went against the grain for me, as I hate motorbikes, to me they are noisy, smelly, dangerous things, but Jason had taken all the tests and passed so I gave in.

I was worried every day he was out on it (as any caring parent would be). One day he said he was going to be staying on at work to do some overtime, to finish an important order, so, "Expect me when you see me."

As there were no mobile phones around then, that's what we did. Good job he warned me or else I would have been thinking he had been hurt somewhere on his bike, it was 48 hours later when he came home, totally exhausted. He had worked straight through for that amount of time. He came into the lounge and sat down.

I went into the kitchen and made him a cup of coffee, when I came back, he was curled up fast asleep. When Tony came home he helped Jason up to bed and we left him to sleep. Jason has never slept for more than four hours at a time since he was born but this time he slept for a full 12 hours.

When he finally came downstairs, he told us he would like to go to college and learn Motorbike Mechanics but he didn't know where to start. We looked and found there was only one college doing this particular course and that was miles away in Bridlington. He applied and was accepted for the next intake, which was three months' away. Now we had to find somewhere for him to live — the course was only for a year so that wasn't too bad. We found him a room with a family near to the college; we went to see them to see if we liked each other and that they could indeed accommodate Jason. Despite this family having three children of their own everything seemed fine so we agreed and got things settled. We paid six months' rent in advance for Jason's room by selling Tony's new car, which gave him enough left over to buy a little Mini.

Before Jason started college, we decided to take him on another holiday to the Canary Isles. This time we went to Gran Canaria. It was totally different from the last island we had been to. This one was really busy, there were shops, bars and cafés everywhere. It was lovely and warm though and we really had a great time, once we learnt to ignore the locals trying to sell us stuff all the time (they were very pushy). And we spent a lot of time killing cockroaches, they seemed to be everywhere and were SO BIG... ugh not going there again.

While all this was going on, Colette was still living with her friend and protector Darren, whom she was now having a relationship with. She told us she was pregnant and didn't dare tell Darren as he had told her he didn't want kids. Well, too bad. We said she had to tell him and if he didn't want to stand by her then we would. Darren still had the Mohican haircut, still had tattoos, still looked fierce but when it came right down to it he was a "pussycat." He surprised Colette and said, "Of course I will stand by you, after all it's my child too."

They also put their name down on the council housing list, which surprisingly came up with a 2-bedroomed flat for them nearer to all of us. It didn't take long to get them settled in as they didn't have much to start with. Colette was a good housekeeper and with her artistic talents she soon had some good decor on the walls. She really did have a gift for art. We still wanted her to go to Art College but she always said she wasn't good enough which was rubbish — she could paint and draw almost anything and it was always in perspective. Maybe one day she will realise that she really does have a wonderful talent, and now she had a baby boy. She painted some fabulous murals in the nursery.

Three weeks before her 18th birthday their son was born; I spent a lot of my time now going and helping Colette. To be honest she didn't need too much help — she was a natural mum, but oh, so young. Darren too seemed in awe of his new son. I don't think I have ever seen Darren smile so much.

Although I was worried about Colette being such a young mum, I have to say I did enjoy being a granny and Tony's mum adored her great grandson — she bought him lots of presents and wanted to see him most days. Unfortunately, that only lasted six months as she got cancer of the throat and was dead within a few weeks, so she didn't see him for long.

We tried to help with the funeral arrangements but Tony's youngest sister informed us all, she was in charge and she wanted no one helping her. She wouldn't even allow Tony to see his mum and say goodbye. His dad never said anything against his daughter as she could do no wrong in his eyes. Although Tony was hurt, he let it go as he said she was, "too distraught losing Mum so quickly."

After the funeral, we were both a little down, now Jason was in college and Colette was in her flat, we were living totally alone for the first time in 18 years. It was all strange and there seemed to be a big void. The children had been the centre of our lives, our time and energy had been mainly focused on them and now they were no longer there relying on us.

So Tony and I decided to take another holiday abroad. We went back to Fuerteventura (for some strange reason I cannot say what, I JUST LOVE that island — maybe it's the total peace and warmth?). We went for two weeks to cheer us up, and it worked. We had a wonderful time again. We met some very nice people and we all went out, car sharing to explore the island. Wow, it was so much bigger than we realised. We were staying in the northern part of the island and we went down to see what the southern part was like. Well, it was like being on another isle. The only language spoken was German (erm, this is a Spanish isle). Good job Tony could speak German or else we wouldn't have gotten the food or drinks we wanted. I guess they don't have disabled people in Germany either, or else they don't give a damn about their needs.

Now at this time in my life, I could still walk but needed a stick. My energy didn't last long with continued use, so, going to the toilet there, was really bad for me and Tony. The ladies' were down three flights of stairs underground. I was ok going down, but poor Tony had to lift me one step at a time to get back up. What a nightmare. We were both knackered when reaching the top.

Apparently, the Germans had taken over this end of the island and made it theirs. They had built some fabulous houses and everywhere you looked, there were fir trees growing. They had planted thousands of them. It was all so very green, not at all like the northern end where it was more like a desert. But at least the Spanish had disabled facilities for the tourist.

We both loved this island and we made enquiries about moving and living here because I really did move so much easier and had much less pain. It would have been idyllic but the laws state you have to have at least £30,000 spare after all expenses have gone out in your bank and at least £250 per week coming in, so that ruled us out. I was living on disability pay. It comes to nowhere near that and of course Tony would still need to work which brought up a whole new set of rules we couldn't meet. So that dream went out the window. That of course was in the early 90s. I have no idea what the criteria would be for living there now.

Back home again and trying to settle down to our routine, I was only going to the church office twice a week now, in the mornings, as there were more people giving their time. I went to see Colette and the baby most days too but didn't stay long. I have never been one to impose myself on to people too much, and Colette was doing well on her own — she didn't need me hanging around. Needless to say, she did want some advice on bringing up a baby. I told her there is no rule book as such, just a few guidelines — we parents have always had to play it by ear — just go with what you feel is right for you and your child. Of course, I could tell her our experiences when bringing her and her brother up, but even some of that is not relevant, as each child is unique and what's good for one won't necessarily be good for another. The main things I think are essential for making sure baby is happy is to be well fed, dry, and loved. Well, Colette sure gave plenty of that.

Now it was all well and good visiting people for an hour or so at a time but that leaves a lot of time alone as Tony was at work all morning and out doing church work most afternoons. One day when we were relaxing Tony said, "You know we said we should like to live on the coast when the children had left home?"

"Yes, I remember," said I. "We wanted to live in Norfolk somewhere."

"Well, how would you like to live in Torquay and be near your mum? I know you're worried about her being alone now your dad's gone and I know I can do church work down there." Now that was something to think about. It was true, I had been worried about my mum, every time we talked on the phone she'd tell me how lonely she was. I told Colette what her dad had suggested and she said, "That sounds like a great idea. It's supposed to be warmer down there and it's not too far to drive down and visit." So the seed was set and it grew as these things do. I must admit the idea of living on the coast was really tempting but, I had a new grandson and Colette still seemed so young to be left. Yes, I knew, she could cope and was doing a marvellous job.

I guess I was just procrastinating because I didn't want to let go and leave them. Anyway, we finally made the decision to sell up and go. The trouble was the house market was still in the doldrums and people came to view offering such silly low prices we just refused. Then I said to Tony, "If the house is only going to sell for a low price, how about asking Darren and Colette if they would like to buy it (if we put down the deposit — thinking there was no way Darren would take on that sort of commitment)?

There you go, I was wrong! He said he would love to buy it, if he could get a mortgage, which he did. I was still sure he wasn't a stayer, so we had a clause put into the contract that should they split up, Colette would get the £15,000 we had given her for deposit before anything else was taken out. Darren even agreed to that!

Torquay

So it was settled — we were going to live in Torquay staying at my mum's until we found somewhere to rent. That was another first. We had not rented since being married. I didn't think it would be any different but, oh, how wrong I was.

There are many flats and apartments in Torquay because apparently folk really did come down here to retire, as it is known as 'The English Riviera'. Personally, I was still not sure this was the place for me as there are steep hills everywhere. I certainly could not go walking about. I went everywhere in my car and shopped at the most level areas I could. It was also the only town in England I knew that did not recognise the Disabled Badge for parking. I was often told to move on by the traffic wardens. One even came out with the gem we have all heard in Mito land, "You don't look sick, why are you using that badge?" It was on a good day and l was not using my stick!

Our first week was very dramatic on moving to Torquay, like I said we were staying with my mum until we found a place to stay; we were looking through flats for rent when Mum's phone rang. It was my brother Paul. He was very distraught and asked if we would go over as he had just found his wife Linda, dead in the bath!

I drove Mum over to his place and when we got there, there were police, ambulance, doctors coming and going from the house. They had gotten Linda out of the bathroom and were still trying to resuscitate her but it was too late, she was gone. Mum and I were trying to console the children and Paul was being interviewed by the police in another room. I was given the job of ringing up Linda's other daughter in Leicester to tell her the sad news. Thank goodness her husband was there as Tracey thought it was a joke, because today was her mum's birthday and there is no way she would be dead! Would anyone really say that as a joke? I realised she was in shock because she had been talking about her wedding plans just a few hours ago with her mum.

Paul was questioned for hours by the police. In the end, it seems they were satisfied with his story, which was — he thought Linda had been in the bath too long and went up to see if she was okay (they were getting ready to go out and celebrate her birthday). There was no response and the door was locked, so he broke it down and found her under the water. He pulled the plug and then dragged her out and tried to resuscitate her but couldn't. He called the ambulance who automatically call the police in those circumstances. It seems the time of death was exactly the same as her time of birth and this was her birthday. Spooky.

We found out later Linda was very depressed because they were going to have their house repossessed. Paul had lost his job and they were struggling. She couldn't live without her house, and she had refused help from the doctors. What a shame she seemed to love her house more than life and her family. How sad is that?

There was an inquest of course. Linda's parents and her sister all blamed Paul for not realising she was ill. Even though he had and she had refused help, that didn't make any difference — they totally blanked him out after that. According to them, he should have dragged her to the doctor's and made her tell everything. Yeah, right. As if! The funeral was taken back in Leicester where she was born and the rest of her family lived.

After the shock of all that we went back to looking for a place to stay. If Mum had her way we would be here forever! No way. We needed our own space again. We eventually found a lovely two-bedroom apartment with sea views over the bay. There was a balcony so we could sit out and enjoy the view anytime it wasn't raining. Now there's the problem - I came to this town mainly because of Mum but also because it was supposed to be warm, sunny and dry — hah! Well, let me tell you WET and warm is more like it. The sun didn't shine that much, even our new doctor said, "Why have you come to live down here with your bad chest? It's the worst place for being humid, and people with breathing problems should not be here."

He was a really nice doctor and actually took an interest in me and my disability, so much so he suggested a consultant friend at the hospital I should see who specialises in neurology and muscular problems. When I said, "That would be great," he wrote to him.

We had an appointment a few months later and I finally got to meet someone who genuinely wanted to find out what was wrong with me and told me there would be many tests to go through if I was still willing — well of course I was. The dream of finding out what I had and hopefully finding a cure was all I thought about. So we went on a voyage of discovery. I went to Derriford Hospital in Plymouth for tests. I went to Torbay Hospital for tests. I went to Frenchay Hospital in Bristol for tests, which included blood tests, lung tests, heart tests, muscle biopsy, electric tests, and so on etc., etc. I felt more like a pincushion than a person, but I gritted my teeth through the pain and told myself it was all for a good cause, still dreaming of the cure!

After all the months of tests and examinations, I finally found out what was causing all my troubles during my lifetime. I have spent many years in hospital and had many operations, tests, biopsies etc., but until 1993 nobody could tell me what it was I was suffering from. My neurologist came into the room, he said, "I have good news and bad news. The **good news** is, we now know what you have is called Mitochondrial Myopathy, the **bad news** is there is no cure for it at this time."

The neurologist explained how I would gradually go downhill but said it could take maybe 40 years to do so. It depended on how physical I got because we are exercise intolerant, which means I can do some gentle exercise but should never force myself to do more.

Well, that was a double whammy for me as I always dreamed of them finding out what was wrong and then curing me. To my shame I went downhill into the **land of sorrow and depression.** Thankfully for me I have one mighty wonderful husband who has always been there for me and he managed to bring me back to the real world. It took him many months, **but lucky for me he is a stayer.**

I was told this was a rare disease and only about 100 are known in England to have it. Everyone I ever met has never heard of it, they mostly thought I was 'putting it on' or 'being lazy' as nothing shows to say I have a disability. How many times did I wish for something that showed so people would know and treat me with some understanding?

So now I knew what was in store for me. During the fog of depression Tony thought it might be better if we got a ground floor flat as he was having to help me up the stairs every time we went out. It was a good idea. We decided to go back to owning our home as we had lots of problems with our landlady. She would come when we were not in and use her own key to have a look around. That is a violation of privacy so Tony changed the locks which she didn't like one bit and made it her business to come as often as she could for an inspection and disrupting our lives.

We found a really nice flat on Babbacombe Downs. There were lots of shops all around us. It had two bedrooms, lounge, kitchen, dining room, bathroom and a lovely walled garden. Perfick!

Colette had been given an intensive driving lesson course from us, so she too could drive down here to visit. She passed it but told us she wouldn't be driving down yet as she was having another baby. A few months later she had another son — so to get a flat on the level made even more sense as they would come and visit quite often and stay for a few days at a time. Darren once said, "Why is it every time we come down here it rains, is it me?" I smiled and said, "No it's not you, it rains here more than anywhere else," or so it seemed to me.

Torquay was a really nice place when the sun came out (and if you're fit, going up those hills), but as far as I was concerned it didn't come out enough. I would often take Mum out for a drive along those narrow, Devon lanes. She was like a little excited child saying, "Oh, look at that," or, "Did you see those beautiful flowers?" "Er, NO Mum, I am driving along tiny twisting lanes!"

As soon as we left Torquay behind, the sun shone. We often went up onto the moors; it was like being in another world. You could see for miles on a clear day. The Dartmoor ponies would come up to see if we had any apples. None of them seemed at all shy. Devon is a special place that's for sure.

One of the reasons I worried about my mum was that after dad died she seemed so lost and alone with no friends. She got bored very easily, so I thought going down there we would be able to have many days out shopping or sightseeing and for a while we did. Then she suddenly found some friends and also got a job in a hotel, so every time we went out had to be when she had finished work which meant most of the day was gone. Hmm.

Tony finally lost his dad. He had been ill for a while. We had visited him at Christmas and knew he didn't have much longer before he died and although he wasn't close to him, Tony still felt the loss a lot and he said, "Now I am an orphan."

What shocked us a lot was the church people AGAIN, as Tony had carried on the work down here and visited many people when in distress. But when he needed help himself NOT ONE PERSON CAME FORWARD. In fact, the only time we got a visit from the minister was when they wanted money for the roof restoration project. Can you believe that?

I think that was the beginning of the end for Tony and the church. He has never lost his faith but decided to dedicate the rest of his life to looking after me, as there were some noticeable changes in my condition. Now I was finding it more difficult to stand up, indeed I was falling over a lot more. One day Tony had gone out for a walk so I decided to sit in the garden by the pond and watch the fish. It was one of those rare sunny days, it was so calming and peaceful — when the phone rang inside. I tried to get up to go and answer it. Unfortunately, I lost my balance and fell face first in a prickly bush — ouch, that really hurt. Worst of it was, it took me ages to get out of it and then had to crawl to the seat to get up off the floor. I was scratched up over my face, arms, and my knees. The effort it took to get back inside the home made me feel so tired, the next day I couldn't move. I was really stiff. Tony put me in a hot bath, which did help loads and gave me plenty of pain meds but it still took me a week to feel anything like my normal self.

He said, "Right that's it, I am never leaving you alone again." He thought it was his fault for leaving me but he really does need to get out and have a break. I made him a promise that I would not go outside again while he wasn't there. Of course that doesn't mean I sat still all the time and one day while Tony was out I thought I would go into the kitchen and get started on the dinner.

I was holding a bottle of tomato sauce. I turned around to add some to the gravy when I lost my balance, still holding onto the sauce. I fell straight down on my bottom; the sauce flew out the bottle and went ALL over the walls so when Tony walked in all he saw to start with was red smears where there shouldn't have been any and me on the floor (he thought it was blood splatter — a 'Dexter' moment I think). Oops. After he got over the shock he said, "It seems I just can't leave you alone for long." But of course, he did, because I couldn't bear the thought of him staying in all the time when he loved going for walks along the coast.

There are some really nice walks for the able-bodied around Babbacombe. He would take his camera and took some wonderful pictures so he could share his walk with me when he got home. We had to wait for them to be developed as the digital camera wasn't within our price range yet. Speaking of which, the first mobile phones started to come on the market. We did get one of those eventually as we thought it would be helpful for me. It seemed really big and clumsy. The only place we could get a signal was to go over one road and stand in the middle of another — fortunately it was a very quiet road. The calls were very expensive so we didn't use it much, but I always took it out with me when I was driving.

We bought a manual wheelchair so that I too could go onto the Downs and enjoy the sea views. I didn't like the way people came up and talked to Tony about me as if I wasn't there. Sometimes I would look up at them and say, "Excuse me, I can hear and speak for myself," so then they came up close to my face and shouted as if I was deaf or retarded.

It really annoyed me how ignorant able-bodied people are towards anyone with a disability, so after a few weeks I told Tony not to bother taking me out. I would rather stay in home and read. We put the wheelchair away for maybe using if and when I might need it.

We carried on like this for a few years, enjoying the visits from family. They loved their free holidays, and we travelled up to see them now and again. During this time both our children got married. I hardly ever saw my mum anymore as she had found lots of friends and was still busy working.

Worse than anything else though, we noticed our little dog Gizmo was behaving strangely. As I have said before he was my shadow and totally devoted to me. He was not eating when we put his food down.

He just looked at it and started whimpering. When he was out for his toileting he just sat and stared at the wall again whimpering.

He would come inside and do his business. We took him to the vet and was told Gizmo had senile dementia and could be given tablets to help but it would only do so for a few weeks and the best thing we could do for him was to have him put to sleep.

I felt so shocked to be losing my best friend and stayed right to the end holding him crying my eyes out. It was so strange living here without him. Tony and I decided to move over to the East coast where we both felt happy and there weren't hills everywhere. So our flat went up for sale. Amazingly it only took a few weeks to sell.

Norfolk

We had decided we would buy another mobile home when we finally got to Norfolk. We stayed with Colette while we were looking, as it wasn't so far to travel. I hadn't realised Colette and Darren were having problems but it seemed they were and things came to a head while we were there. Darren said he had had enough of being married. He took the kids out into the garden and told them he was leaving but he said it loud enough for the neighbourhood to hear. Their youngest was just six years old and he thought his dad was leaving because of something he had done to make his dad mad. How do you explain to a child that young that Mum and Dad just can't live together anymore?

Eventually after looking at many mobile home parks, we found what we were looking for, a double unit on a quiet park on the edge of a small village, surrounded by fields. It was so peaceful and the best thing was no children were allowed to actually live on the park — it was for over 50's only. Grandchildren were allowed for a two-week stay at one time. **Perfect!**

The unit we bought needed some TLC and we got the builders in to sort it all out for us, including a new tiled roof and double-glazing. When they had finished, Tony built a veranda at the front and back so we could sit out. The park manager built a long ramp so I could get in and out without any struggling with steps.

Most people, friends and family, could not understand how we could leave somewhere as nice as Torquay in the South for a place in Snettisham on the East coast. Well **it was easy** — although the wind did blow more, the air was fresh AND it didn't rain nearly every day. In fact this area of Norfolk is known as the driest county in England. We both found it really warm. Most evenings found us sitting out on the veranda with a drink or two and looking up at the stars. It was amazing, there were MILLIONS of them. There was no light pollution here. I can honestly say I had not seen this many stars since I was a child.

We have always loved Norfolk. Most years as the children were growing up we had our holidays somewhere on this coast, mainly in Cromer. That is the most wheelchair/disabled friendly town I have ever been to. Every shop I went in was accessible.

Both Tony and I noticed our breathing was much better too. He has suffered from asthma all his life and I have damaged lungs from all the pneumonia I had had. Being able to breathe easier can only be a bonus as far as I was concerned. The doctors were even helpful and interested in Mitochondrial Myopathy. They found it fascinating as none had ever heard of it.

Our medical records were still in the old format of being hand-written, and it took them a while to read it all.

One thing did bother me and as all Mito sufferers will know about it, is the problem with bowel movements. I used to be in agony and sometimes would sit on the toilet for an hour or so. One day the pain was so bad that Tony called the doctor. He gave me an examination and told the nurse to give me an enema then because I had been bleeding. He made an appointment for me to go and have an endoscopy. I went and I actually could see my tubes inside, they were very clean, which is good. There was no sign of cancer, much to our relief. The doctor gave me some medicine to take daily to soften my stools so I didn't have to go through this agony anymore.

We are now in the early 2000's and I thought I was in heaven. This place was so idyllic. I sat on the garden swing listening to the birdsong. There were even a few skylarks around. It was pure bliss. Tony could go for a walk most days. We were only a mile from the sea so he often walked to the beach; sometimes he took me in the car but of course I cannot walk on sand so I just sat on a big rock watching the seagulls. There is a bird sanctuary there too. Each day we could look up and see thousands of birds coming in to roost, it was magnificent. A lot were Canadian geese and we could hear them honking before we saw them. It was said there was at least 32,000 coming in every evening to roost. Every morning they all came back over to go to the feeding grounds.

As you might have gathered by now I love birds. They are so very entertaining and some sing a pretty song. We had at least 10 feeders hanging around the garden and two tables. Tony even made a special pond where they could come to drink and bathe. He placed it just a few feet away from the veranda where I sat every day watching them. They all got used to us watching, even when we were looking after my friends' dog for a few days, the birds still came. It was as if they knew we were friendly and wouldn't hurt them. We had many species visiting us, from the humble sparrow, siskin, tits, robin, blackbird, thrush, woodpecker, bullfinch, through to a jaybird, pheasants and ducks.

At night when most birds were sleeping we could hear the hedgehogs visit for their food (we put out dog/cat food). When I wasn't sleeping too well I would get up and sit watching them (they were very good at keeping the slugs away). I even saw an owl or two.

I made friends with the lady next door, though still cautious about getting involved we did seem to have a lot in common, and sometimes we all went to the theatre together in Hunstanton. Sometimes we would look after her dog when she went away for a weekend.

Another thing that happened to me was I went menopausal. Suddenly I was getting hot flushes, which I found wonderful after having years of feeling cold. All of a sudden, I was HOT. The central heating was turned off most of the time (bonus for Tony) and windows were opened. It was amazing and I loved it. There were no more of those horrid periods with all the pains that went with them. There was a down side too, it seemed when the menopause came in the sex drive went out. It was just as if a switch had been thrown and the sex queen no longer had the drive. Tony and I talked about it as I was worried for him but he said he didn't need it anymore either. We had had lots of fun along the way but now was the time for other pursuits.

It really did seem such an idyllic life we had here. We were both very relaxed so WHY did I wake up one morning with a terrible pain in my chest and find it so hard to breathe? Tony took one look at me and called the doctor who told him to call an ambulance as it sounded to him like I was having a heart attack. Seven minutes later they were there and after examining me said I had to go to hospital. I was so frightened, but I said to the ambulance man, "I cannot go into hospital, it's my mum's birthday. I have things to do and arrange," but he said that would have to wait. Getting me sorted was his priority.

So it was off to the Queen Elizabeth Hospital for me. As usual I saw lots of different doctors none of whom had heard of Mitochondrial Disease. I told as many as were interested what it meant and how it affected me. Of course there is always one doctor who thinks he is above all others, I met him.

I know most consultants think they are special (and some really are) but Dr Kumar thought he was the BEST of the BEST. He was the most arrogant man I have ever met — when he came to see me after my heart attack, he said, "You have all the signs of having a heart attack but I need you to do all the tests with the exercise machines." I said, "I doubt that I would be able to do them as I am exercise intolerant." He gave me the strangest look and said, "What makes you say that?"

I told him about Mitochondrial Disease and all the tests I had had and how I couldn't even get on the treadmill. His reply was one we have heard before but it had a kicker to it, he said, "I have never heard of this Mitochondrial Myopathy you're talking about and if you can't be bothered to take the tests then I can do nothing more." With that he walked off. Later one of his interns came up with a list of medications the GREAT man had said I needed to keep my heart at a steady pace, the main one being a statin. At this point in my life I didn't know anything about statins or what devastating effects they can have on people, especially if you have Mito so I took them, thinking the doctor knows best.

Tony and I had seen adverts for home computers and we got to thinking maybe we should join the modern world and get one. That's easier said than done when you don't have a clue about them and of course neither of us did — so when we saw an ad for a package deal for £99.00 of a computer, printer and scanner we thought, 'Why not try that and see how we go?' Well, it seemed okay, we managed to get online and work most things out but after a few months we noticed the machine was going very slow. Of course, we had no clue, so we got someone in who did know. He said the memory was full — we had something like 256MB RAM and 512MB memory [not too sure of these numbers but it was very near] using Windows 95 and thought that was a lot. We had a lot to learn! We did a deal with him. He took ours and we got a laptop with much more memory and the speed seemed F-A-S-T. Now this sort of computing was much easier for me than the one we had at the office which used DOS, this was Windows 98. The world was opening.

One of the things I found the Internet very useful for was looking for information about my two younger brothers that had been involved in an aeroplane crash (they bought the plane to make getting to customers easier and avoid road traffic). I found out via the Internet just what sort of plane a Beechcraft Baron 55 looked like and according to the police report, '... just as the plane had taken off, a crosswind had flipped the plane over and it cart-wheeled six times before hitting a tree, with the nose pointing into the ground and the tail up in the air.' I went on-line and printed the picture — what a wreck. How my brothers got out alive I have no idea. Mike the pilot escaped with minor cuts and bruises but Pete had broken both hips, pelvis, left leg, left arm and both collar bones. He was in intensive care for weeks — the doctors rebuilt most of his breaks and replaced some with metal rods. They used over 200 screws to help rebuild him. (sounds like the six-million-dollar-man. Ha-ha-ha). As you can imagine it took him a long time to get back on his feet but he too is a fighter and refused to give in.

We had been here in this idyllic place now for four years and I have to say it's one of the most wonderful experiences of our lives. One day whilst sitting in the garden listening to the birds as usual, it suddenly went very quiet. No bird song or anything then we heard a low growling kind of noise. Tony looked over the hedge to see what was going on and there was a huge machine. It was some sort of digger. It seemed they were going to build houses on the fields surrounding us, that was very bad news. They started by stripping out all the trees in the hedgerows, which meant insects and birds would lose their homes and shelter from the winds.

Then they dug up the fields to mark out where the new houses were going. It was pure devastation and to top it all, the rats started to come into our gardens as their habitats had been destroyed. They were not afraid of us either, they blatantly sat around looking at us looking at them. It was very creepy. It also meant we had to stop putting food out for the birds for a while until we had the rat problem sorted.

One morning I woke up and saw Tony had a black eye. I said, "How did you get that?" He looked at me and said, "You punched me in the eye last night!" Well, I knew I had started thrashing around more but didn't realise I had turned into a bully. I was devastated and we decided it was time to get separate beds. I have to say I had reservations about it to start with but once we got them I realised we had done the right thing. Although I still wasn't sleeping well at least now I wasn't disturbing Tony anymore and doing damage to him. And now we had more space to ourselves as we had a three-foot wide bed each instead of sharing a 4' 6".

I had noticed too that I was not getting about easily any more, in fact standing up was becoming extremely difficult. I was feeling so tired and worn out, I went back to my GP many times but he said he couldn't find anything else wrong and my heart seemed to be ticking over nicely (which if I am honest is what I was worrying about). After having a problem with your heart, I think you are always on edge and wondering when the next whammy is coming. I certainly was and I remember after Tony had his heart attack we were both on edge for months. So, if my heart was all right then it must be my Mito. It seemed to me as if I was slipping downhill faster than I ever thought and there was no way to stop it. I was getting really worried about Tony coping with me on his own (never thought about carers) or being left on his own with our children living too far away to help. Colette asked, "If you could get a place to live in Leicester would you come back?"

Well, that is something we said we would never do, but with all this building work going on around us we thought — maybe. I said, "Well if you could get us somewhere near you and Jason then we might consider it." We wrote to the Leicester County Council and asked if we could go on their waiting list for a bungalow with wheelchair access. They said we could after filling in all the forms BUT it would be at least three to four years waiting, so we thought we had lots of time to get used to the idea. I had just started using a wheelchair when we went out anywhere. I couldn't use one in the mobile home as all the doors were much too narrow. It looked like we would have to move anyway before much longer. My slide downhill was getting quicker. It seemed I couldn't stand without losing my balance and falling and the pains were so bad in my muscles, what few I had left.

Sometimes I cannot believe how things turn around so quickly. It seemed I had seriously underestimated our daughter. From the day we got the news we had been put on the waiting list for a bungalow, to the phone call from Colette saying she had found one suitable in the right area took just THREE weeks. There was Tony and I thinking we had three or four years to become adjusted to moving, now it seemed there was a big rush on to get us back to Leicester.

Of course, we had to go and view the bungalow and see if it was wheelchair accessible. It was and so we went to sign the paperwork. While Tony and I went back to Norfolk to pack and sort out, Colette and her boys spent most evenings decorating the bungalow, getting flooring laid and hanging curtains.

It was all ready for us to move into on November 24th. Our GP said something really nice when we went to say goodbye, he took both my hands in his and said he would really miss us going to his surgery and I made him feel humbled because I was always so cheerful. He gave me a hug and a kiss as we said goodbye. That made me fill up.

> Worrying is a waste of time. It doesn't change anything. It messes with your mind and steals your happiness.

Full Circle

So now here we are, back where we started, two miles outside of the city centre, in the town of Braunstone where both Tony and I were born and spent many of our younger years playing or visiting.

We have moved into a bungalow that is warden-controlled, which means there is an emergency alarm system fixed to the wall with pull cords in different rooms. Plus, a warden actually comes round once a week to see if we are all right and if there are any problems with the property. They also help in sorting out all the benefits we might be entitled to. They are very helpful and cheery, so when we got a leak in the roof we told the warden who reported it and it was fixed in a couple of hours. Great service!

There are a lot of older people living around us too so mostly it's quiet. The only downside to living here is the college and school just around the corner — the children do make lots of noise when coming and going from there. I guess we were that noisy too at their age but I don't remember it. We certainly did not use the foul language they do now and we had respect for our elders. I don't think youngsters today know what respect is.

I was given a new neurology doctor when we came back. I had to wait six months for an appointment. When we finally got to see him, he seemed interested in Mito and actually knew about it. We went through all the meds I had been taking and he was appalled when he heard I was taking statins. "No wonder you have gone downhill and are suffering pains. They are the worst thing you could ever take, stop them immediately."

He never did any tests apart from blood tests. He said, "There is no point, I can see just looking at the muscle wastage there is nothing to be done. Just talking to you I realise you are both aware and have adjusted to your situation, so there is nothing more I can do for you." And that was that.

Now the GP was a different matter. Apart from the fact the GPs never stayed long enough to get to know the patients, NONE ever seemed interested at all in Mito. Until three years ago — we got a very nice doctor who at least listened and did read some of the information we printed out. It seems to me not many medical staff take us really seriously because it is such a rare disease and there just aren't enough of us to make the difference.

Our bungalow is really tiny but it does have a lovely little back garden — we asked permission to put a conservatory on the back to give us a little more room. It was granted. I chose one with floor to ceiling windows, so when sitting in while it's raining, it's just like sitting in the garden without getting wet. I can sit and watch the birds without disturbing them or me getting cold. PERFECT!

We are also very lucky to live five minutes away from a VERY BIG park. It has two lakes on it and while walking/wheeling around there, you cannot hear any traffic noises. It is a lovely place to go for peace and quiet. There are many ducks, geese, swans, etc., so I take plenty of food along and feed them. Some even come and take it from your hands! I love it.

So, all in all we are settling in nicely. Both Tony and myself have taken up painting again. Tony prefers using water colours on paper and I prefer acrylics on canvas. We both joined a couple of artist websites so we can learn more and see how others do and give each other encouragement. There are some really helpful people out there and thanks to the Internet everything is so much easier.

I even got a commission to paint Canterbury Cathedral. That was very difficult but a great learning curve.

Now, there's a saying called Murphy's Law which is to the effect that, "Anything that can go wrong will go wrong." And so, it was when in 2008 I had a fall and broke my arm late at night. The 24-hour emergency callout we have wasn't working as a lorry had accidentally pulled the wires down in the street, so Tony rang for an ambulance.

I was stuck on the floor for over an hour until help arrived. Then because of the position I was in and I couldn't help push myself up, the two men that came didn't have the right equipment to pick me up. They had to call for another ambulance that did have the equipment, 20 minutes later they arrived.

It took five people to get me up as they are no longer able to pick people up (thanks to Health and Safety regulations).

We had to wait another 30 minutes while a device was brought in to help raise me and because my arm was broken in a bad place they couldn't get a good grip on me — what a nightmare. I was shaking so badly, not sure if it was from the cold tiles I had been sitting on for so long or the fright or even the pain. The ambulance man had given me gas and air to breathe in which did help take away the pain and when he said did you know you were sitting on a huge spider I laughed and said good because he's the reason I'm down here. And so, off to Leicester Royal Infirmary (LRI) Accident and Emergency (A&E) we went, where I was seen by numerous medical people. The doctor finally decided it was broken so badly they couldn't put a cast on and just strapped it up temporarily. He said he would look at it in a day or so!

Eventually I was taken to a ward after being seen to and had it strapped up. I never realised just how much I used my arms until I no longer could. It was terrible. I couldn't do anything without help and the nursing staff were totally unsympathetic. They told me to stop being lazy and get up to go to the toilet when I asked for a bedpan. I tried explaining about Mito and the difficulties I have with standing up and walking with two crutches (how do you do that with a broken arm?). How I have never been able to lift my head off a pillow or slide up a bed amongst many other things I am unable to do — there were few nursing staff who took the time to listen or help. They brought my meals and put them on the table then left it at the bottom of the bed out of reach and later came and took it away saying, "Oh. Weren't you hungry?"

One staff nurse told me I had to use the commode and get myself out of bed even though I had explained many times. This time though Tony was there and he helped me out and put me on the commode. There was a big argument between them as the nurse told him he was not allowed to help me. He told her he had been helping me all our married life and was not going to stop now. She was fuming. It was one of the worst times of my life. I have spent many times in hospital and I have to say this is the worst experience I had ever had. Tony knew I was very upset and not being looked after so he told them I was going home and there would be complaints going in about my treatment. And we did — there was plenty to complain about.

We had apologies from management etc., but it was too late as far as I am concerned. I will never go back to that hospital.

Something happened to me after breaking my arm, suddenly I was terrified of standing without holding onto something. I kept thinking if I let go I am going to fall again and maybe break something else. All my confidence and bravado had gone, I was a quivering wreck. Now was the time I finally took to my power chair full time. I had had it for a while and only used it when we went shopping. I never wanted to use it as I thought it meant I was giving in to my illness instead of fighting it. Tony had to change the controller over to the other side as it was my right arm I had broken and couldn't use the controls that side. I was realising I wasn't giving in but being sensible as I couldn't fall over in the chair. I could also look up when we were out and see things I could not see before as I no longer had to watch every step I took. Tony didn't have to worry about me so much either. Bonus!

There was still so much I felt unable to do or had the confidence for. The social services were helpful. They gave me a hospital bed so I could raise and lower myself, plus a commode so I didn't have to struggle to the toilet at night. I found using a Zimmer frame did help me when I tried walking.

Because I couldn't get the power chair in the bathroom very well they also arranged to have the bath taken out and installed a wet room. It included a toilet seat raiser with arms, which I have to say is amazing. Just by pressing the button the seat raises me up to a standing position, much easier for us both. They said it would all be easier for Tony having all this done when he washed me, but, oh! I do miss having a bath — it was the only place where I could go and lay for an hour and be PAIN FREE. The hot water was just so soothing.

Ever since my accident, Tony has been doing all the cooking, cleaning, etc., plus looking after me all the time. He dresses me every morning and undresses me and puts me to bed every night, although at this stage I could still get up to use the commode on my own. But it was getting harder. If I got up more than once a night my legs would go wobbly and I had to make an extra effort to concentrate on standing. I really did try not to disturb Tony at nights, he deserved a good rest after the busy days.

Wishes Do Come True

When I was diagnosed with Mito in 1993 and the awful truth dawned on me, I was a very sad and frightened woman. The doctor told me it was a very rare disease with no cure and he had only heard of approximately 100 more like me in England. Although I have a very caring husband and loving family, I felt SO ALONE and made a wish that I could at least meet another Mito person who might know just how I was feeling, as they too might be feeling the same way.

In August 2009, I had an e-mail from the UK Ambassador for the UMDF (United Mitochondrial Disease Foundation) Mr Rowland Dicker via my art website, asking me if I would like to join a Mito group as he was trying to make contact with more of us. Well, at first I thought it was a wind up, then I realised it was for real and - HEY, at last contact with someone else with this disease — a wish come true.

I did reply of course and have never looked back. Through the Internet I have met and made friends with many more MITOVIANS, who I discovered all felt the same way — that they were alone. Of course we're not and hopefully we have managed to help each other through some very tough times, I certainly have benefited from the caring sent out over the airways.

Now, on July 16th 2011 (my 63rd birthday) it was really wet and windy but my daughter and her husband Ian came and picked Tony and I up at home and took us in their car down to the county of Somerset - 173 miles away, for a special birthday treat — we were to meet up with Rowland for a meal and a chat. The restaurant was booked two weeks in advance so we knew just what we were having and they prepared the place so that the toilet and table were accessible for my wheelchair. I was SO EXCITED.

There we were going down the motorway in the pouring rain and I felt a pain in my chest. No, I can't let this happen, not today. Foolishly I tried to ignore it, after all I have had this lots of times and if I sit quiet it goes away. It did, for a while.

We arrived at Rowland's door and there he was at last, standing tall and proud and very pale. He asked if we wanted to go in for a coffee but we thought it would be best and less tiring if we went straight to the restaurant. So he got in the car and off we set. Now, what amazed me was how easily he chatted with us all, as if we had been best friends for years. Rowland directed Ian the best way to get to the restaurant in the town of Chard, which is about 20 miles distant from his home. It takes about 40 minutes driving, over the hills to get there — and after finding a disabled parking space off we went for our meal, AND THE SUN CAME OUT. YAY! I was hoping to be my usual jolly self and have a real good laugh, but the pain came back and I felt very unwell. But this was my special day and so many people had gone to a lot of trouble for me, so I never let on how I truly felt — just that I didn't feel too good.

Simon and Tracey, the restaurant owners, had prepared everything for our best comfort, even going that extra mile and ordering my most favourite cake of Black Forest Gateau. The meal was superb and the company was fantastic. Young Rowland was a perfect gentleman and very good company and I was so pleased that we had finally met face to face. Another wish come true.

All too soon it was time for us to go home. I was sorry to have felt ill whilst we were having a good time, but it was just a wonderful experience meeting as we did and I want to THANK EVERYONE FOR A FABULOUS BIRTHDAY and making my wish come true. I would do it all over again if possible without the heart pain!

Much later, back at home, after spending a sleepless night after our long return trip, Tony called for an ambulance. They came, examined me, and said I had to go into hospital where again after more tests and seeing lots of different staff they all came to the same conclusion, I had had another heart attack. This time I got lucky, they sent me to the special Heart Hospital only a few minutes up the road from where we lived. Unlike that other hospital, the staff in this one ALL seemed to care, and most were even interested in my Mito. In fact, one student nurse wanted to do a thesis on the subject. The Internet it seems got a lot more hits on the search engines for Mitochondrial Disease during my stay there.

I was moved to three different wards while there as my condition went from critical to stable to observation and in every place I felt like the staff really did care. Nothing, it seemed, was too much trouble for them.

Only once did I see a grumpy nurse. The ward I was now in (a four bedded) had some great patients, there was Mavis opposite me, then Jenny and Hilda, we were all having a great laugh and being a bit silly ('tis true), but this nurse came in with such a stern look on her face and shouted, "Will you all be QUIET! Don't you realise this is a hospital?" Then she stormed out again.

Well, it did go quiet for about three seconds, then I looked at Mavis, she looked at me and we just burst out laughing again. Mavis said, "Ooh-er, do you think we have upset her?" I was still laughing and said, "Of course we realise we're in a hospital - DUH! We're getting enough injections and blood taken out of us, does that mean we can't have a laugh?" Too bad. We didn't let that incident bother us. In fact, everyone else who came into our room said what a lovely happy lot we were and what a pleasure it was to come in.

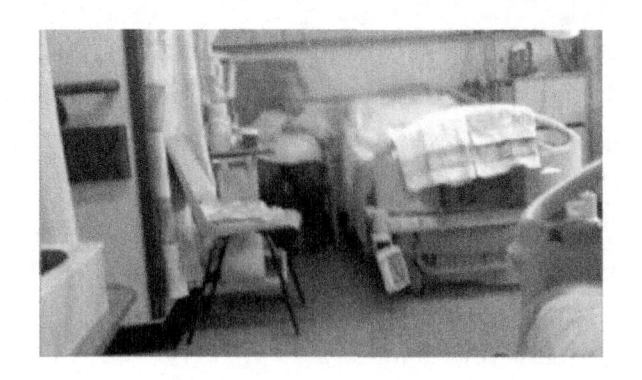

Mavis was just like me, small and roundish. There she was, fast asleep. She was looking forward to her 80th birthday and we could both talk forever. We had a lot in common, including that twinkle in the eye. Had we lived near enough to each other we could have had even more fun but she lives 15 miles away from me and neither of us have our own transport, so the phone gets used plenty.

After all the tests were completed and the doctors were sure there was nothing else they could do for me, they told me that my left ventricle is not pumping the blood through properly. I actually saw the movement on the ultrasound — it kind of fibrillated instead of positively opening and closing, that scared me. The doctor said it was probably caused by my Mito weakening it. All they could do was give me certain medications to help the blood flow easier. However, what scared me more was the day they did an angiogram on me. (An angiogram is a test that's used to find out more about your heart. It can help to show if blood vessels called coronary arteries, which supply blood to your heart, are narrowed or blocked. If they are, it can show where and how severely they are affected. It can also see how well your heart is pumping blood.) As they were doing the procedure I started to feel really peculiar and I heard some shout out, "We're losing her." Everything stopped for a few minutes. Did I pass out? Not sure, but they managed to finish. The result was my heart is not blocked but that valve is damaged which they could do nothing about it. They said I could go home.

Which was another test — for the first couple of weeks I felt really vulnerable, but a heart nurse came and answered all my questions putting me at ease.

So that's how our lives seemed to be now. I do have to say when I was involved in a painting I did lose track of time and didn't worry or think about anything but my painting, and had Tony not been alert I would hardly have eaten or drank anything during those engrossing times. During my stay in hospital I got 11 commissions so I was kept very busy after coming home. Trouble was they all wanted their paintings finished before Christmas. It kind of takes the fun away for me when I am on a tight schedule, so I sorted them into an order of priority and got on with it. I am pleased to say everyone got their painting on time, even the two going to Hungary.

Our landlords had decided we needed a new kitchen. We had been given some choices of colour, work tops, and unit styles, they even arranged for a special pull-out work top that was lower for me to use in the wheelchair. When it was all finally fitted I could become useful a little and help Tony to chop and prepare food. Now it's my job to make the sandwiches when we have them. Yay! Go me!

Soon after Christmas, I noticed that once again things were more difficult. One night I tried to get to the commode and fell, so I had to shout Tony awake to come and get me back up, which he did through very blurry eyes. I felt terrible for waking him and when I was back in bed I made the decision to not get out any more during the night, so I have gone full circle with something else as I now wear nappies (incontinence pants) at night. I hated them at first and was really indignant at having to have them put on, but gradually realised it was better than falling during the night. It is also true they do keep dry so you're not feeling wet all the time.

Which brings me to another problem a lot of us suffer with but are too embarrassed to talk about. Most Mito's suffer from gut problems which lead to many complications. Mine was mainly constipation, which I have suffered since birth. I used to sit for up to an hour and half trying to go, and actually fainted many times as the pain was so bad. Tony and sometimes Colette were always there to stop me from falling and hated to see me in so much pain but were helpless as to what to do to help. Of course, just being there was reassuring but it seems my muscles are not always strong enough to push when needed and so it built up, which led to haemorrhoids. Believe me it's no fun sitting in a wheelchair when they flare up. One time when it was really bad I trawled the Internet to see what help was out there and came upon a booklet with many different ideas in, so I bought it downloaded it to my desktop and I tried one of the simpler treatments and sure enough it works. Now for the last year I have been free from any problem and have not had to have poor Tony standing holding my hand.

I also seem less able to lift my arms at all so having a drink takes more effort. I use a baby cup with a handle on both sides and as it's plastic it is lighter. Even so sometimes I have involuntary jerks and spill it. When in bed Tony puts the lid with a spout on so I can drink without spilling it as I cannot lift my head up from the pillow. Same with eating. I have special tools with thicker handles on to help me grip them but of course some of the food goes on walkabout and never makes it to my mouth.

The choking and swallowing seems to be getting worse too. I seem to get trouble swallowing my own saliva and even breathing in seems to bring on a bout of choking. It's all very frightening and embarrassing, a few times now Tony has had to give me a thump to help move food not going down. The worst thing about falling is how quick I go down, there is never any warning. It seems like my knees just fold under and I'm down before any of us realise it, which is the reason I try and concentrate when I am actually standing up. Having osteoporosis does make you more wary, breaking bones is definitely no joke.

Nowadays I cannot move very much at all, apart from my arms, when I'm laying down. Maybe my scoliosis has gotten worse therefore making it more difficult to move. When Tony puts me into bed he makes sure I am comfortable and that's where I stay all night.

Of course, I don't sleep too well and lie there for hours. Thanks to modern technology I have my iPhone for listening to music or lately talking books. Sometimes I watch TV on my iPad; so at least the nights don't drag as much as they used to. When the morning comes and Tony gets me up he gives me a good massage to bring back the circulation.

Speaking of which could I write all this and not mention that wonderful part of technology — SKYPE on the computer? For quite a few years now it has brought me much closer to my friends and some family. I find it truly remarkable to be able to speak with people from all over the world. Sometimes the time differences make it more difficult but so worth the effort. To have a conversation one to one and be able to see each other is really good if you mind the camera on — some don't and that's fine, of course we very often have a group chat. Some special people have shared their highs and their lows with me as I have with them and to those I wish to say a BIG THANK YOU for being there... again you know who you are.

Goodbye Peter

Today my brother Peter who has always let you know exactly how he feels and has never pulled any punches as far as I know, and was always ready to give you a hug, came to see me all the way from sunny California. He couldn't have chosen a worse time weather-wise, it has been wet, windy and cold. Considering it's supposed to be summer but he wanted to come and say goodbye to me as he has cancer all through his body and the doctors have told him he only has a few months left on this Earth. His first words when he came in with his true, impish smile were, "Hello darling. You're looking well considering the doctors said you wouldn't live past 20 years, so what do they know? Ha-ha-ha-ha!" Then he said, "I will wait for you at the gate and we can walk into Heaven together!"

We had a real good long chat and reminisced over old times, good and bad. I told him I was writing this book and some of the content. He was very shocked at some of it and sad too that he hadn't known, so he could have maybe helped and given me some support. He said he could understand me hating my brother for what he did.

I told him I don't hate Chris, I hate what he did. Pete looked surprised and said, "Wow. You're amazing." I don't feel amazing, I feel sad for any person who stoops so low. Then again maybe he picked on me because Dad had treated him so badly and I was 'Daddy's Girl'.

Pete also said how much he admires me for all I have had to go through and yet still keep smiling. As far as I am concerned, we have two choices when faced with trouble, we either let it devour us and go down miserable or we fight it and stay as happy as possible. I choose the latter. He also thinks I am very brave to be so happy when I am stuck in this wheelchair — again, I have no choice. I am certainly not going to give up. He says the thought of spending the rest of his life in a wheelchair is too much and he couldn't do it, so " ...it's a good job I got this cancer and will never find out…" But I think when we have to face this sort of thing we always find the strength to cope. And whether he realises it or not, he is doing exactly the same. He keeps smiling even though he too suffers great pain. I love him and admire his strength as much as he does me.

Then he saw a photo of my grandchildren and we talked about them for a while. Showing each other different pictures of our grandchildren we both agree being a grandparent is better than being a parent. The joy the children have given us is immeasurable and it is such a shame we won't see them grown up.

It was a strange time and him telling me he doubts he will see me again because of the cancer sounded unreal. He won't give in, but as the pain gets worse and the medication gets less effective, we doubt he will have a choice. We had a big cuddle and he said goodbye with a sad smile on his face. I haven't cried yet, I dare say that will come later.

So it did on the 8th of December 2014. I had the phone call from Michael: Peter passed away peacefully with his wife, brother, son and daughter all by his side. Then I cried. I often say our tears are mainly for our own selves because we will miss the one we loved so much and the only upside I can see is at least Peter is in no more pain and suffering. As he died in his beloved California it meant I was not able to go to his funeral, had he had one. But Peter being Peter donated his body to science to help up and coming medical people. So, the few family left over here got together and said our farewells to Peter with a small memorial of our own. After Christmas when family came back here to England we had a bigger memorial service held at the Leicester football stadium. He was an avid fan and strong supporter of the team and in their Garden of Remembrance there is a plaque with Peter's name on and the words, "They think it's all over. Well it is now." He would have loved that.

Still getting over the loss of Peter came another. Our mum passed away on the 29th January 2015 aged 87. She had been unwell for some time and was actually in a Home because she could no longer look after herself. It was another unpleasant phone call Michael had to make to me. Once again because she lived so far away I could not go to the funeral. But I did attend, thanks to the Internet as where the service was held had Internet links. It was set up for more of my family to attend in our home. It was very nice to have them here too, giving me comfort over our loss.

Some people say the Internet is the worst invention ever because of all the bad things happening. I personally do not agree. Yes, it's true there are many who abuse it and cause misery, but it has also brought much happiness and knowledge into our lives. For me it has brought many new friends who all suffer the same illness. Now I never feel alone and afraid of what's to come. All I have to do is send a message to a friend and there they are talking with me on the screen via Skype and cheering me up. There's also the shopping. Now, I never have to worry about wheelchair access as I can go to practically any shop in the world and get just what I want or need. I think used in the right way the internet is AWESOMELY LIBERATING… and I love it. I also thank Steve Jobs for Apple Macs, they are incredibly easy and nice to use. It was a great loss to the computer world when he passed on.

As I have said earlier I am having more problems standing up and near the end of March I had another fall. All I had to do was take three paces from my bed to my wheelchair when down I went. Tony was holding me so I almost pulled him on top of me. I fell straight on to my bottom but the pain came from both knees and my spine. It was agony. There was no way Tony could get me up so he called our daughter and son to see if they could come over. Someone also called the ambulance in case I had damaged my spine. The children got there first and supported me until the ambulance crew arrived. After examining me they said I had to go to the hospital for ex-rays etc. to see what damage was done. Off to A&E we went. I must say things had changed a lot from the last time I was here. The staff were very attentive and efficient and even while I was waiting for one doctor then another someone came and made both Tony and me a drink and some sandwiches. After all the examinations, tests and x-rays it was decided there was no damage. I had put my back muscles into spasm and all I needed to do was to go home and lay flat until the pain went. That was all well and good but how was Tony supposed to look after me now. I simply could not move without causing great pain. We needed help.

We rang the Social Services and told them our plight. Two days later someone came to assess what was needed. (Have you ever tried eating, cleaning your teeth or going to the toilet flat on your back?) It is very difficult when there is pain with it. We needed a ceiling hoist to help lift me but I was told, "We don't provide those, the only hoist we can give you is a portable one."

We already had one of those but there just was not enough floor space to use it. Colette and Tony had tried but when they turned me it just tipped over, the response to that was, "I can go back to the office and see what they can do but it will be at least eight weeks because we will have to get a survey done and permission from your landlord before we can fix anything up."

I got very upset then at the prospect of waiting eight weeks before I could get out of bed, so I suggested getting one of the portable ceiling hoists in. Again, she said, "We don't do them." Tony said, "Well, in that case we will get our own; not sure how we will pay for it but we'll get one."

As it happens my brother Paul used to work in that line of things and when I told him what the Social Services said he replied, "Don't worry Carol. I will sort something out, you won't have to wait weeks either. Sure enough, five days later he came to our home with a gantry ceiling hoist which has a frame going over the bed from wall to wall. He fixed it up in 15 minutes and he showed us how to put the sling on and move me from the bed to my wheelchair. My back was still painful but it was such a relief to get out of bed for a short time. As I got stronger I was able to be hoisted on to the commode for relief. Of course, when Social Services learned of the hoist they said, "Now you have that you won't need one from us." Over the next few weeks I had physiotherapists, to help strengthen my back and legs. The occupational therapist also came to see what else I could have to help and then I got carers to come in and help as Tony was finding it all a bit stressful. Now I have two carers twice a day to help me get washed, dressed and up into the wheelchair in the mornings and to undress and put me to bed in the evenings. Tony said he felt like he was letting me down but I said, "You have looked after me for over 40 years and you have done your share. Now it's time for you to relax a little. There's no way you have ever let me down."

It took us both a while to adjust to having carers do what Tony used to do. We have gotten into a good routine and most of the carers are really good, while some are just good and a couple have been… not so good. So I guess we have been lucky when I hear stories of other people having carers that are bad.

We are not sure how long they will be coming but I was told they will come for as long as I need them. At the moment they are paid for by social services but one day I expect there will be a review and another look at my incomings to see if I can pay for them myself. Until then we are just carrying on. The weeks are flying fast and our routine has become quite steady until…

The week started off quietly, Tony and myself thought "That's the way we like it." Sunday and Monday passed normally, Tuesday Colette always comes to see us and she brings her dog. This routine has been going for five months. Nothing new there, however Tony has been losing his balance quite a lot just lately (he won't go to the docs to find out why). Anyway, this is where our peaceful week changed.

There we all are sitting in the lounge having a cup of coffee when the phone rings. Me being the nearest thought I would answer it. However, Tony got to his feet and said, "No, I will get it," then lost his balance and fell on top of the dog. The dog did what any dog would do, lifted his head up — Tony's arm went into the dog's mouth and it caught in the dog's sharp teeth. Tony still proceeded to get the phone … it was for me … when he handed the phone over, blood was pouring down his arm. Washing it under cold water never stopped the flow so Colette rang for an ambulance. Then she took the dog home and came straight back. A few minutes later the paramedic arrived, took one look at Tony's arm and said, "You will have to go to hospital, that wound is too bad for me to fix." He put clean dressings on and called for the ambulance which arrived a few minutes later.

Tony was admitted to hospital and was told he would possibly need a skin graft so he wouldn't be coming home tonight. He had to see a plastic surgeon in the morning. If after the operation, everything went well, then he could come home. The surgeon came and said he would like to leave the wound open now the bleeding had stopped, before he decided what to do next. Tony won't be home this night either.

So in all my 67 years on this Earth I have never been completely alone at night. There has always been someone nearby (I guess I have been lucky enough to have that happen as I know many people who have not had that privilege). So when Colette locked me in as she was going home, I felt very strange knowing there was no one in the house with me. Kinda scary too.

By now the carers had arranged for me to have more care. Tony, when he came home, would not be able to do as much as he had before. Thursday came. Colette had permission from her boss to work from my home so she could be here if I needed anything. Of course I did as I can neither use the kettle, food areas or the toilet on my own. Her company was great even though she was feeling guilty about what had happened. The third night I was locked in again and as I had every night, I talked to my friend Rowland on Skype for at least two hours. He made the nights less lonely and frightening. Thank you Rowly for being a true friend.

Friday. They decided Tony would have to have an operation but still not sure what they were going to do to cover the wound. In the end, it was decided they would try and stitch it up, if there was enough skin to do so. If there was not enough then they would do a skin graft taking some from his thigh. All this was going to happen in the morning (Saturday) so now another night alone. I forgot to ask the carers to leave the telephone on my bedside table just in case it rang and of course it did for ages and ages. I guessed it was Jason. I used my mobile phone and called him, asking 'Have you been ringing me? If so I cannot reach it, it is in the hall.' He just wanted to know how I was coping.

Here we are, Saturday at last. Tony rang. He was just going down for his op and would ring me later. He did, sounding all fuzzy after the anaesthetic. They have managed to sew him back together. Now it's a waiting game to see if the stitches hold. If they don't, he may still have to have a skin graft but he was definitely coming home today. Jason was at work and Colette was miles away finalising the dog's paperwork, so Tony had to wait until she got back. He doesn't mind as he's still groggy but the ward has to close soon and cannot do so until someone picks him up. He is not allowed to get a taxi. When Colette got back I rang Tony.

And so there I sat in my lounge all alone in my wheelchair talking to Tony on the phone telling him Colette was on her way to bring him home from the hospital when the doorbell rang. I eventually got the door open, phone in one hand, wheelchair controller in the other. There stood two policemen. One said, "Hello, are you Mrs Williams?" "Yes," I replied. "Can we come in and talk to you for a few minutes?" I let them in. This is how the conversation went:

"Where is Mr Williams?"

"He is at the hospital. I am talking to him now on the phone. If it's about the dog, he has gone back to the kennels."

"No madam it's not about the dog although we do know about it. We need to talk to you about something else, so when you have finished talking to Mr Williams then we will talk."

"Anything you say to me, Tony should hear too."

"No, it's best if we wait for you to put the phone down."

So I said goodbye to Tony and hung up and said, "Ok if this is not about the dog, what is it about?"

"It's about your son Jason."

"What about Jason, is he all right?"

He looked me in the eyes and said, "I am sorry to tell you but Jason passed away this morning at 7.30am under suspicious circumstances. I can't say any more at the moment as it is still being investigated."

Well, I was dumbstruck for a moment. It felt as if all the blood was draining down and out from my body. Then I realised he said 7.30am this morning and I said, "NOOOOOO that's not right, it cannot be my son. You must have got it wrong."

"No, we haven't, I am truly sorry to say it, but it's true."

"NO, NO it is not, I was talking to Jay this morning and we have texted each other."

"What time did you do that?"

"I don't know, it's on my phone."

"Can I see that please?"

"My phone's in my bedroom."

They get the phone and I get to my messages —shaking so badly I can hardly scroll up but there it is —12:11. Then they ask me what Jason's date of birth is and one calls their HQ for verification. The other asked me if I had a photo of Jason. I pointed to one on the shelf with his family, the two policemen looked at each other and said, "That's not him. We are so sorry for upsetting you Mrs Williams truly, truly sorry," and with that they walked out, leaving me alone feeling so many things all at once. Upsetting is very understated, I was also relieved, sad, confused and angry.

I have seen this happen on the TV many times but they were just programmes. This was real. Surely the police don't go around doing this in real life? But it seems they do. I was sorry to hear a young man had died but also very glad to hear my son was still alive. As I sat there thinking over what had happened, Tony came walking in. Well, I was so relieved to see him back home as he put his arm around me I just burst into tears.

I did eventually get a letter of apology from the chief of police and a big bouquet of flowers. That did not stop the pain and anger I felt. I have lost my faith in the one establishment I have always trusted.

Life took on a new turn for me, as Tony was diagnosed with type 2 diabetes. Some of the tests showed he also had cancer. He had to spend more time in hospital while they did tests. The carers were coming more to help me but I was still locked in on my own at night. It was not a thing I had ever had to do and I felt very frightened and vulnerable being left helpless in bed from 7.30pm to 9.30am.

Then we were told of a care home with a difference that might suit us and as it had only been opened a few months there might be places still available. Tony hated the idea of moving, but he too was worried about me being left alone, so we made an appointment to view the flats. It was an assisted independent extra care home, meaning you still have your own flat and independence but there is care 24/7 if it is needed; I will need it, now Tony cannot do so much. I have to say when we looked around we were both pleasantly surprised at how well run it seemed to be. There is a shop, a hairdresser, a cinema, library, a craft room, a lovely garden, a restaurant and all the staff were really friendly and helpful. We went through all the procedures and assessments from the council, the social and the home itself. They all agreed it was the perfect place for both our needs and we could move in a few weeks' time.

Oak Court (The Hotel)

The day of the move is kind of blurry as everything was done for us by our family. Paul had come up from Devon to do our packing and bless him he stayed over and did most of our unpacking too (I know we could not have done it on our own). A big THANK YOU to all who made our life easier. We are settling in.

Our main meal is cooked and waiting for us in the dining area. The little shop sells bits and pieces, if they haven't got what you want they get it for the next day. The hairdressers I have been to a few times now, it's the one luxury I have had to do without for years. Now I am going to indulge. Often. Of course there are a few things I have got to get used to. As this is a communal building there are certain rules, some of which affect me. I am having a few problems with some of them…

Like the rule that carers cannot apply any cream to my person unless it is on a prescription, with detailed instructions from the doctor where, when, and how often it is to be used, and more to be used when required, (so all my creams the other carers used to help keep my skin from drying out cannot be touched).

Like the hot water is set at 40% in the taps so no-one can get scalded, 40% is like lukewarm you cannot wash greasy pots in that temperature and saying boil a kettle to add to the wash is ridiculous, that would be much more dangerous!

Like no onions, garlic, peppers or meat on the bone! All because someone choked on one. And other things that can be too much for a delicate person to have. why does everyone assume that once you get past a certain age your 'Delicate' Good grief anyone would think we have no mind left to make such decisions. excuse me but isn't this supposed to be a restaurant for us to choose our meal? 'No,' I'm told.

Management decided it will be too costly we only have the kitchen open for lunch between 12noon-1:30pm and we have to pay for our meal whether we have it or not. So if you go away for a few days the meals will still have to be paid for! If you come later than that, all cooked food will be in the bin. It's all to do with health and safety. Red-tape again. I know some people need these things but the majority of us still have common sense and to throw the food away is just wrong.

We had an open day in June to celebrate this wonderful establishment, with many upper managers, councillors, press and a celebrity by the name of Angela Rippon. She was very pleasant and managed to speak to most people, which was amazing as there were around 200 walking about. I managed to present her with one of my paintings. She asked me if I like it here. I told her I call this 'The Hotel' as it is so good and I love it.

My young brother came over from Hawaii where he lives (he asked me to go live over there but I said I prefer this place). He stayed in the guest suite for a couple of nights, as did my good friend Rowland on another occasion. Both were impressed and are coming back again for another visit one day.

So far, I have joined a few groups, like the gentle exercise and the quiz and ball games; had lots of fun and laughs and even won a few prizes. Woo-hoo! I am also Secretary of the Association Committee for the residents. Now, that has been an eye-opener. I never realised how much work there was do for 70-ish members. Sometimes it feels like a full-time job, and here's me thinking I had retired. Funnily enough, I love it. Plus — people have asked me to paint a portrait of someone they love and Tony has been asked to paint a few pictures. The art classes are going really well, most who turn up have never painted before and are now in their 80/90's and loving it. All have been surprised at their abilities. We even made a calendar for next year using the art paintings they had done.

After being here for many months I have come to cherish my carers, they are simply the best. Nothing is too much trouble for them and they help do things for me that Tony usually did.

Tony's having more bad days now. Having said that, his hospital check-up was good. They are impressed he's doing so well considering he's not having chemo. It seems the cancer has not grown any more. It hasn't shrunk either, but he is keeping a positive attitude. The HRT injections along with the herbal stuff he takes seem to be doing the trick for now.

People think it strange that we have our funerals completely arranged and can talk about it so openly. It may sound strange but we actually get comfort knowing it's all sorted. The children won't have to worry about anything when we pass. Living here in the Hotel must have put our children's minds at rest that we are well cared for as we see very little of them nowadays.

Here we were, thinking everything is going so well. It seems nothing stays good for long. The higher managers are not happy with the money they are spending on our care and have come up with some stupid new work rota that involves split-shifts and back-to-backs, resulting in tired, weary and demoralised staff not able to do the job so well and hardly seeing their families. Split-shifts should never have come into this scheme. Managers have said, "They will never do them." Well, that's very bad, no manager worth anything should expect their employees to do what they are not prepared to do themselves. I have written to their managers and complained about the loss of staff brought on by their own managers' rigidity and short-sightedness. In this kind of work there has to be flexibility. I doubt it will make any difference but at least they know how we feel, though goodness knows what will happen when most of this caring team have left. Yes, they will get new staff eventually but that is going to take months. What happens to our care in the meantime? Maybe there will be a new team trained up eventually who are as good.

I have written to the CEO of EMHhomes asking them why we are being put into this situation (who passed it down to the manager of Enable who are actually in charge of our care). We got a response and had a meeting to discuss our situation, she told us she has made a big mistake in the financing of our care and can no longer carry on the way we were. It is her mistake but now we are going to have to pay for it... by having less carers around. This was not good enough for us, they have broken their promise of 24/7 care and support leaving us with only minimal care and very little support.

I have written to The Care Quality Commission (CQC) whom we have now met and had discussions with. The officer we spoke to was very surprised by what is happening and will make a report to his superiors and letting us know when this has happened. I have written to the BBC and told them of our plight, they too said they will get in touch and hear our story (I wonder!). The tenants want me to go to the newspapers with our story, I prefer to wait and see what happens with those I have written to before going down that road.

I have requested a meeting with the county council and asked them for an explanation on our care package and the changes. If nothing positive comes from all that then I guess it will be more agency care and less continuity, something I positively hate. and was not why I came.

I won't give up the fight for what we believe in. We can only hope that with positivity and endurance all will be to most people's satisfaction. We will never please everyone. Recently we had our Summer Fête and it was hard work, there was minimum staff on and it was difficult setting up stalls without the help of carers (something they used to do) now we have to do it all, most of us have health problems and it was very hard work, but we did it and managed to raise £519.99 for entertainment nights.

Tony and I never came here thinking we would need to do so much work, we thought we had actually retired to concentrate on our Art full time and to be cared for when needed.

It seems we and a very few others are the only ones able and willing to stand up for the rights of all the tenants so we will carry on and do our best for as long as our energy holds out, funnily enough we seem to have more energy at the moment with all we are trying to do, I hope it lasts.

My brother Michael has just been for another visit to 'the Hotel' from Hawaii and again as we walked down the corridors he said, "It is still a lovely place you live in 'Cas', you're so lucky to live here… and of course he's right, despite all the problems it is lovely and we are lucky.

So here we are two older codgers as we while away the time, going for walks when it's fine, enjoying each other for as long as we may be granted, and through it all we have done many things, met many people and would not change a thing. Through good and bad times, life has been and still is great. We have been truly blessed.

Mito's — How Do We Do…?

The question is: "How do we do?"

"Do what?" I hear you say. Well, manage with the little things people take for granted. And I ask because a friend of mine was visiting and watched me do my hair before we went out and she said, "You are amazing! How you do that?"

"Do what?" I asked. She replied, "Your hair."

I have never given it any thought before as I grew up finding ways to be independent, and Tony has never assumed I cannot do things as he knows how I value my independence. He waits until I ask for help.

So now I have been thinking of those things we do differently from 'Normals' as in non-Mito sufferers, and try to explain how, but to be honest it's not easy. I am sure we all have our own ways of doing most things. These are just a few of mine.

So, when I 'do my hair' I usually sit at the table to support my elbows and arrange a mirror in front so I can see what needs doing. If no table is available I just support one elbow with my other hand as I have never been able to lift my arms above my head. It's all a matter of planning.

Cleaning my teeth has become so much easier since the invention of the electric toothbrush too. I just support my elbow at the sink while sitting in front of the sink and let the brush do the hard work while I gently guide it around.

Standing up from sitting has always been a struggle but I put my hands on my knees and somehow push up at the same time, walking my hands up my thighs until I am standing.

Walking used to be busy as I was always looking for the lowest kerb when crossing roads and watching every step I took so as not to trip up. And of course, always looking for the shortest, easiest route possible.

Going up stairs I had to put one foot on the stair then pull on the rail as I pushed on the other foot putting them both together before repeating the process all the way to the top. If there was no rail I used the wall for support and pushed with my shoulder. Using a stair lift is very good. Nowadays though stairs are a NO-NO. If there is no ramp I don't go, simple as that.

Getting up from the floor was a challenge. I had to get on my knees, crawl to a chair or step, get my bum on the seat then stand. If there is nothing to lean on I was stuffed. I remember walking to work once and I fell at the side of a main road, cars whizzing past one side and shops the other. The shopkeepers looked and laughed at my attempts to ask for help from people passing by — they all looked at me as if I was a drunk or demented. Then a friend saw me and came to my rescue. It was all very humiliating for me, and all because of the invisibility of this illness.

Turning in bed is the same, when I could do it, I usually inched my way over with little jerky movements and pulled on the headboard until I reached the desired position. I have a gadget to help lift my legs into bed. It's a long-handled loop that I hook over my foot and then pull it onto the bed. I also have a long-handled gripper for picking things up. Great stuff. Heh!

I find there are two important words for MITO movement and they are: **Support** and **Planning**. Every move I make is planned out in my mind before I attempt to do anything. It is something I have been doing so naturally I didn't even notice until it was pointed out. Maybe growing up with it has been more helpful for me than for those who suddenly find they have Mito and are having to adjust. And 'support' — make sure you have support when weight-bearing.

I accepted years ago that I would one day be wheelchair bound, but I have never given into it, only it finally got me a few years ago (the good thing about being in a wheelchair is that

I don't have to worry about falling any more). And I can go faster too! (Strangely enough I was talking to Tony about it just a while ago. I asked him if he ever thought all those years ago that he would be doing so much to help me now. His reply was, "I have always said I will take care of you from day one and I meant it." We just take one day at a time and cope with whatever life throws at us.) Well life has thrown quite a bit at us and we just do what needs doing as best we can. Tony sure has saved the government a lot of money by being my unpaid carer. If he couldn't do it I would need at least six carers a day and of course they are on full pay. I am not sure what they earn per hour, I don't know if it's more than our pension. Still we manage and are happy and so each new day brings on a new challenge of, "How do I do that?" Of course there are times when I know I am beaten and cannot manage to do something, then I swallow my pride and ask for help.

An example of how I plan getting on the loo. First, the MANTRA: 'Think before you move.' I put the wheelchair in the right position near the rail, switch off motor, then hold onto the rail. Next, stand up making sure to keep knees locked straight, then turn, always holding onto rail with one hand and wheelchair arm with the other. Stand up straight, pull dress up (this is the worst bit as I have to let go of rail so I really do need to think carefully), so concentrating on standing, knees still locked, skirt up, sit on loo (I don't wear pants as I never got them down in time and wet them). Stand up when finished by pressing button on seat raiser, when at the right height, hold onto rail, turn and flush toilet, then still holding on and still concentrating keeping the knees locked, edge backwards onto wheelchair seat and sit down. Then and only then can I relax again.

These are just but a very few of the things we have to adapt to and like all Mitovians everywhere there are many things we have to do to cope that we do subconsciously and don't think about how we do until someone says — "How Do You Do That?"

Some Of My Favourite Songs

And now a bit more reminiscing from me with a tiny few RELEVANT SONGS FOR MY LIFE. These are just the first that came into my head of the songs that have meaning for me. There are far too many to name them all. My music list on my computer has 1,781 on the last count. They are just the ones I have bought, there are many, many more I like but have not bought.

Everybody Loves A Lover
Doris Day... My given pet name when I was young was POLLYANNA (dictionary definition is "an excessively cheerful or optimistic person")... well that's how I have always been and will carry on being so.

You Raise Me Up
Brian Kennedy... This is for Tony, who has indeed raised me up soooooo many times, and never once has he complained in all our time together.

There You Are
Willie Nelson... A soppy song of remembrance of how things were when two people in love are no longer together... I'm just a big softy.

Jezebel
Frankie Lane... I was called this many times during my rebellious times. Hehehe...

I've Had The Time Of My Life
Dirty Dancing... Yep, despite all that has been thrown at me during my life I can honestly say, "I Have Had The Time Of My Life.... Woohoo!"

In My Car I'm The Driver
Shania Twain... That's how I always felt when I used to drive, and oh, how I loved to drive... NO backseat drivers here please.

Nothing I Can Do About It Now
Willie Nelson... Well it's so true whatever has happened, there really is nothing we can do about it, just go with the flow and ENJOY.... Have no regrets.

Nights I Can't Remember
Toby Keith... Oh, yes crazy days and full nights of naughties, what a way to go, life has given me plenty to remember.

You're Still My Girl
Raymond Froggatt... Here is another song that I feel was just for Tony and me, and after 41years of being together, I really am still Tony's girl. How lucky I have been...

Thank You For The Music
Abba... Indeed, A BIG THANK YOU, for what would we be without music. It has been a BIG part of my life. I love all kinds of music, it has cheered me up made me melancholy, made me feel loved, and how much joy and fun it has given is priceless.

My My Time Flies

Enya… How true is that? My time has flown so fast I still cannot believe I have made it to my 60's already, and only one year to go for my 70th… I still feel soooooo young and able... I don't think I am ever going to act my age…

Man's Best Friend

And so to the question of should I have a dog or not to keep me company, here is our personal experience of mans' best friend. It is said so often and I quite believe it's true, mans' best friend is his dog, and if you find the right one and treat them right you will be rewarded a hundred-fold, from my own experience there really is nothing to beat it.

Our best friend was a little Papillon (the butterfly dog). He was truly devoted to me, he made me laugh when he played silly games which he did quite often. When I was feeling poorly he would come and put his head on my lap and give me a look that said, 'Get well soon, I don't like to see you ill.' He greeted me with so much pleasure when I arrived home, he would bring me presents, usually one of his toys), as if to say, 'Here Mum, I love you and want you to have this.'

He didn't like dog food, apart from biscuits, so he had the same meals as we did, even when we went vegetarian. He followed me everywhere, even to the loo, and he would sit by the bath when I was having a soak.

When we went to bed at night he would sleep down by my side but very often Tony and I would awaken with him laying between us, head on the pillow snoring! Our dog was named "Gizmo." He was a lapdog, full of fun and vitality. Although he hated going for walks, he loved dashing about on the park. He has been gone 11 years now but I still miss him and have never wanted another because no other could take his place.

There are many decisions to make on getting a dog. After deciding you REALLY want one, and can you afford one, not just the buying but also everyday costs, you have to decide what sort of dog you want big, middle, small; long-haired, short-haired; pedigree or mongrel? Does it need long walks like a greyhound or no walks like a lapdog? Do you want just a guard dog or a house pet?

Some dogs cost a lot to keep with special diets, vets bills, flea treatments, grooming. Will you mind if they moult all over your treasured furniture and carpets? Getting them house trained can be a slow process and some vomit a lot too, could you cope with that? There are many aspects to look at when deciding what's right for you, for obvious reasons I do prefer the smaller dog but whatever reason or size you have... if you treat them right they will indeed be your BEST FRIEND.

And I do believe they can be beneficial. For instance, our neighbour had a severe stroke years ago and has not been able to speak apart from one word. After giving it sincere thought her husband finally decided she could have the small dog she always wanted. He told her, "You had better call it Dave," because that's the only word she could say. However, after just a few weeks she has spoken several more words and can move a little better too. Little Dave sits on her knee most of the day and gives her lots of affection. I honestly believe dogs understand us far better than we do them and their love is unconditional.

There are many aspects to look at when deciding what's right for you, for obvious reasons I do prefer the smaller dog but whatever reason or size you have... if you treat them right they will indeed be your BEST FRIEND.

Walking Sticks

The reasons I finally got myself a walking stick.

How many of us with Mito refuse to use a walking stick until it's a last resort? It seems to me that many people I have spoken to about them think they are for OLD people... which of course is a very negative thing to think. They are for anyone who needs help. There are many different shapes and sizes out there. Just look on the web.

A walking stick is very helpful in many ways. All you need to do when buying one is to make sure it is a comfortable height when holding the handle, make sure it is not pushing your shoulder up. It should be a good sturdy one, with a rubber ferrule. There are some that fold up (I have one) but I don't feel so secure with it as I worry it might fold up while I'm using it. The three parts are only held together with a thick rubber band, which I suppose will perish one day.

When you first get a stick it does seem a little strange and awkward. Which hand you hold it in is a personal choice, which ever feels more comfortable and natural. I practiced in home quite a bit before I ventured outside. It soon became one of my best friends.

When I was A LOT younger I used to use my umbrella all rolled up tightly to help me as I got fed up with being pushed and told to hurry along. Comments like, "I wish I had all day to dawdle like you," or, "Come on, move. You're SO lazy." Oh! How I used to wish my disability showed so people would leave me alone to go at my own speed. (My dad used to say that I had two speeds — "dead slow and stop.")

I carried on using my brolly until my children were born. Then I had something else to hold on to, first their pram and then the pushchair. Of course, in home the furniture used to help me keep my balance. As the years went by I realised it was getting harder to walk without help. My GP and then Tony suggested I get a stick. He even went with me to choose one. I have to say it's one of the best buys I have made. Not only did it help me to keep my balance and give me something to lean on when I was really tired, BUT people actually asked me if I needed any help carrying stuff comes in handy when something is out of reach or you need to give someone a prod, and even trip that ignorant person up who thinks they own the path!

Even now I spend my time in a wheelchair I still have my stick nearby... just in case!

What is Mitochondrial disease?

Mitochondrial disease occurs when there is mitochondrial dysfunction usually due to a genetic mutation (spelling mistake in the genetic code or a bit missing) involving either the mitochondrial or nuclear DNA.

There are a large number of mitochondrial diseases some of which are shown on page 164 and mitochondrial disease can affect babies shortly before they are born, to people developing symptoms much later in life. Mitochondrial diseases usually affect tissues which are highly dependent on energy and this includes the brain, heart, and muscles. Many patients have involvement of several different tissues, although in some, a single tissue may be involved, for example deafness or blindness.

Mitochondrial disease can affect patients of any age and often present with different organs involved. This makes it very difficult to determine how many patients have mitochondrial disease. We do know for example DNA mutations which predispose people to mitochondrial problems are present in about 1 in 500 of the population although many of these people will not get any symptoms!

Ehlers Danlos Syndrome (EDS)   Chronic Pain
Gastroparesis   Migraines   Dysautonomia
Oesophageal Reflux Disease   Osteopenia
Pregnancy Complications   Chiari Malformation
Postural Orthostatic Tachycardia Syndrome (POTS)
       Hydrocephalus   Fragile Blood Vessels
        Raynauds Syndrome   Fibromyalgia
              Dental Issues

Scoliosis

Vision Issues

   Depression   Hearing Loss

   Osteoporosis   Aortic Dissection

   Cloudy Memory   Chronic Fatigue

   Easy Bruising   Mastocytosis

Upper GI Dysmotility   Irritable Bowel Syndrome
        Tethered Spinal Cord Syndrome
      Chronic Intestinal Psuedo-Obstruction
            Early Onset Osteoarthritis
       Low Muscle Tone and Muscle Weakness

Imagine trying to run
an entire house on a single
+(Battery)-
THAT is Mitochondrial
Disease

Printed in Great Britain
by Amazon